A FADO
FOR MY MOTHER

Um Fado para minha mãe

(Title of Portuguese song)

OTHER WORKS BY SARAH LAWSON

Poetry

Below the Surface and Other Poems
(Loxwood Stoneleigh)

Translations

The Treasure of the City of Ladies
by Christine de Pisan
(Penguin Classics)

A Foothold in Florida
by René de Laudonnière
(Antique Atlas Publications)

A FADO FOR MY MOTHER

Sarah Lawson

LOXWOOD STONELEIGH
BRISTOL

First published by Loxwood Stoneleigh in 1996

Designed and typeset by Falling Wall Press Ltd, Bristol
Printed and bound in Great Britain by BPC Wheatons Ltd, Exeter
Cover printed by Doveton Press Ltd, Bristol
Cover photo by the author: *Paving stones in the Praça dos Restauradores, Lisbon*
Front cover inset by Charles Porter of Danville, Indiana: *Fern Lawson and Sarah Lawson in 1948*

British Library Cataloguing-in-Publication Data
A catalogue record for this book is available from the British Library.

ISBN 1 85135 023 3

Loxwood Stoneleigh
St Andrew's House, 125 North Road, Bristol BS6 4AH, England

I

The plane swoops down through the clouds and the turbulence joggles us until we begin to come out of the white fog and glimpse the country below us. We have flown south for two and a half hours, but we might as well be landing in London again for all the improvement it has meant in the weather. We come in low over red-tile Latin roofs, lower and lower until it looks as though we are going to land on them instead of an airport runway. I remember these tile roofs and the low flight over them, but the airport has changed. It's much more modern than it was seven years ago. The walls are faced with marble and a little fountain burbles and splashes for arriving passengers.

I have a recurring, irrational fear that someone will ask me what I'm doing here in Lisbon. I imagine a young woman sent out by some department of the Tourist Authority. She holds a clipboard and approaches people in some public place like the airport or a large square in the city. I can almost see her. She is a university student or a recent graduate filling in with a part-time job and speaks good English. She smiles and says, 'May I ask you a few questions?' She ticks off my age and sex and nationality. 'May I ask, please, why you have come to this country?' she says, smiling, pencil poised. When I don't answer immediately she says helpfully, 'Is it perhaps business, or is it a pleasure trip? Do you have friends here?' How am I to condense it into one box for her to tick? However many categories she has, there is not one for me.

I take a taxi to my hotel down in the older section of the

city. I carry on a halting conversation with the taxi driver as he weaves through the rush-hour traffic. When he asks, I tell the driver that I have come from London and that I am on holiday and want to see the important churches and museums, a few of which I name to show my serious intentions. I do not tell him my other reasons. How could I explain them? Still, we have a reasonable conversation, considering my improvised version of his language.

It's already getting dark when I arrive, and there's a slight London-like drizzle, so I don't venture far from the hotel. It's a pleasant, dimly-lit old place in the shopping district. I have my evening meal in the ornate hotel dining-room. It looks like the Spanish Riding School in Vienna, all but the sawdust. It is Georgian blue and white with *bas relief* plaster swags and enormous mirrors. The room is the size of a tennis court, but at this time of year there are never more than four or five other people in it.

I was last in this city seven years ago with my husband, who has stayed in London, and my mother, who is dead now. She enjoyed Lisbon very much. All down the Avenida da Liberdade – down the wide esplanades at both sides of the main roadway – there are intricate mosaic patterns in black and white stones. Each stone is two or three inches square, but in spite of their sharp corners the patterns are arabesques and stylised flowers with many curved lines. The Portuguese must have a highly developed aesthetic sense if they find it necessary to make elegant designs in even the sidewalk paving, but this is a traditional feature of Lisbon. Seeing these charming black and white designs again reminds me of the time when we were here together and my mother admired them.

The next day is sunny and warm. I know I am a typical tourist from the North: I keep marvelling at the warmth and sunshine and palm trees; I keep thinking, 'And all this in February!' The local people seem to think it's normal to walk around in a light coat, unbuttoned at that, in early February.

This is their idea of winter, patronising sidewalk cafés and strolling under the palm trees. In the evening it gets cooler and sometimes it rains. Fashionable ladies put on their fur coats to show each other, but they scarcely need anything so heavy.

I can see the river in the distance and decide to walk down to it and take the ferry to the other side. The hotel is on the high ground of the Chiado, and steep streets lead down to the Tejo, or Tagus. Chiado is the name of the little square, or *largo*, at the end of the Rua Garrett, but it gives its name to that street as well, as a kind of nickname. The Rua Garrett is lined with several smart shoe shops, jewellers' and long-established bookshops.

On the corner of the Rua Nova da Trindade and Chiado there is a shop selling stringed instruments. Glossy guitars and lutes and mandolins are displayed in the window. There is even a ukelele and something with the same shape and the same four strings but very much larger, like a bass ukulele, if such a thing exists. Inside there's a long polished-wood counter, and at night several guitars are arranged neatly on their sides along this counter as a sign that the shop is closed and as an extra advertisement for its wares. In the window, besides the familiar shapes of the Spanish guitar, the ukulele, the mandolin and the lute, there is something I have never seen before. This is the Portuguese guitar: it has a rounded body and a spray of keys like lace bobbins at the end of the neck and its twelve strings are arranged in pairs. The sound hole and the border of the blond body are decorated with intricate designs in mother-of-pearl. When I walk past the shop, trams and cars and pedestrians are reflected in the window along with the headlines at the newspaper kiosk, but the guitars are a motionless continuo of polished shapes under the movement and bustle on the surface of the window.

As a musician, my mother would have been interested in guitars. I never saw her play one, but I know she did when she was a Campfire Girl. She was a music teacher and her instrument was the piano. She played the violin and cello, too, but that was in her student days, or later when she wanted to illustrate something for her schoolchildren. Actually, the guitar wasn't one of her favourite instruments. I suppose that if 88 keys are your standard, six strings look rather thin. In spite of Andrés Segovia and the large guitar repertoire, I don't think she considered it a serious instrument. It was something portable to strum at a picnic when a piano was unavailable.

Music shops always remind me of her, especially those selling stringed instruments. She used to tell how she had gone into a store in Indianapolis and commented on the violin in the window. The point of the story was her mortification on being told that it wasn't a violin but a viola. She had recently received her degree in music and knew perfectly well that a viola is a fifth larger than a violin. 'That's all right, Miss Reed,' the store owner said, 'it's easy to make that mistake when you haven't got the two of them to compare.' I don't know whether her own embarrassment or the store-keeper's tact made a stronger impression on her.

Although we had many things in common, music wasn't one of them. We were both interested in language. When we were here before she was intrigued by the look and sound of Portuguese. If she had studied a modern foreign language she would no doubt have done well at it. As it was, her foreign language was Latin. We went to the same local public high school, but in her day, 35 or 40 years before mine, they did twice as much Latin. She had read Virgil and Cicero in the original, and I haven't. I was always surprised at how much Italian she knew as a result of her music training and her Latin. I remember coming home from school one afternoon and telling her some new Spanish words I had learned, imagining that they would be gratifyingly inscrutable, but she recognised them immediately because they were identical to some Italian tempo indications.

I make my way down the steep streets to the Tejo, which

is farther away than it looked from my hotel window. By leaning out and looking down to the right I could see it, a wide blue expanse with Cacilhas a mile and a half away on the opposite bank. I feel a pang of pity for the old people I see trudging up the hill toward me. Some of them are using walking sticks, but others are hobbling along without any help. There are stooped old ladies in black and lame old men. I wonder how they have survived so long if they have to walk up and down these streets every day.

I come out at the Praça de Terceira, beyond which is the wide coastal highway and Cais do Sodré, where there is a suburban train station and the ferry quay. I buy a ticket for 57 escudos, and soon the car ferry comes. This is mid-morning on a weekday, and it's not very busy. A few dozen people walk off the ferry and five or six cars drive up the ramp onto the quay. They are replaced by five or six cars driving down the ramp and another few dozen foot passengers walking down onto the deck. From the enclosed upper deck you can watch Lisbon become more extensive but smaller behind you and Cacilhas take shape in the approaching distance in front of you. It must seem ironic to the Spanish that the one Spanish river with a good harbour in its estuary flows all across Spain and delivers its harbour to Portugal.

Cacilhas has more steep streets, a shopping district, some fish restaurants. On the way up a street I pass a fire station with a white ambulance out in front. Two firemen are busy scrubbing it. One has a hose and the other has a bucket of soapy water and brush on a long handle. He is energetically scrubbing the side of the vehicle while his companion plays the stream of water from the hose over the hood. A thin trail of soapy water winds back down the street on its way to the Tagus. *Ambulância* is written across the front in mirror writing so that drivers ahead of it in traffic can read it in their rear-view mirrors. On the side is written the name of the district and the fire station, for the fire department is in charge of ambulances. The young men are scrubbing it with all the devoted application of teenagers with their first jalopy.

When the street forks I take the right fork to stay near the river, but I get into some sort of military installation. High up overlooking the Tagus is a squat fortress with the inscription 'Men of steel in walls of granite'. I don't see any men and the walls are concrete, but it is a stirring quotation if you don't examine it too closely.

Farther along at the same height, I come to a pleasant park where you can look west to the high statue of Christ the King, visible for many miles up and down the Tagus estuary, and the 25th of April suspension bridge. I drove across that bridge seven years ago. You go west from the Pombal monument and get on the *auto-estrada* and follow the signs to Setúbal. You climb high up over the river, as high as the hills of Lisbon, but underpinned by nothing but thin air. The Fodor guidebook says that, at a mile and a half, this is the longest suspension bridge in Europe. We went south that day as far as the small town of Aljezur, where we spent the night. The next day we continued to Lagos and Faro on the south coast.

In front of me and down to the right is the city of Lisbon. I can't make out all of its seven hills (or eleven, according to another guidebook), but it is clear that the land is very uneven. Streets and white buildings rise in tiers back from the river and there is the green pine-covered outcrop of the Moorish Castle of St George.

Like Rome, Lisbon was built on seven hills; like Edinburgh it has a castle and an 18th century quarter; like Paris it has a landmark designed by Gustave Eiffel; and like San Francisco it is famous for an earthquake. In 1755 Lisbon was largely destroyed by a violent earthquake which brought down the buildings in the city and caused the anchors of the ships in the harbour to rise to the surface. (I try to imagine what it must have looked like, but I can't; the city across the Tagus looks immovable.) Caring for the survivors and clearing the rubble and rebuilding the city would be a daunting task even in modern times. In 1755 in Portugal the earthquake was taken as a sign of divine displeasure, and in more sceptical countries it suggested that God did not exist or was not paying attention.

Back down by the river I find some archaeological excavations and stop to read the explanatory signs. These are the foundations of a building for salting fish built during the Roman period, which was from the time of Julius Caesar until the 5th century AD. At times like this I feel more than usually North American. Europe is a palimpsest; all our footsteps are on top of other footsteps.

I take the ferry back across the river. Absurdly, the ferry seems familiar now, since I've been on it once before – as Lisbon seems familiar because I have been here once before. I stand outside on the small open upper deck and look at the deep blue river and at Lisbon gradually changing shape. Even here on the water the wind is not cold, even now in February. It's like a summer day in London. This is the bottom, blue, edge of the map. I will start here and work my way up and out, through the winding streets disguising the hillsides. Later this mass of jumbled buildings will make sense and fall into patterns for me. I'll be able to pick out familiar faces, like old schoolmates in a group photo.

Back on the Lisbon side, I climb up the Rua do Alecrim past the monument to the Portuguese writer Eça de Queiroz to the Praça Luís Camões, named after the author of *The Lusiads*, the epic poem about the Portuguese explorations in the 15th and 16th centuries. The nearby Largo de Chiado is named after another poet of that period and he too has a statue, though not as grand as the one in honour of Camoens with its stepped pedestal and other figures ranged around it. Even Rua Garrett is named after the 19th century poet Almeida Garrett. (He has a bust elsewhere in the city, but only the street name here.) It's a more literary district than you can find in most Anglo-Saxon cities.

I have lunch in a whitewashed and tiled restaurant in the Rua Misericórdia. I order grilled swordfish, one of the specialties of Lisbon. Seven years ago we had swordfish, which is how *peixe espada* is translated on menus. It is not the fish with the spear on its nose, but a long, thin fish also called a 'scabbard fish'. The nomenclature is confusing, especially as real swordfish also figures on menus. We had it several times in the restaurant of the hotel where we were staying, and we thought it was very good, whatever it was. Now I am having scabbard fish again in Lisbon. This restaurant is called The Golden Prawn and it's a very agreeable place with its old, low arches. The tiles on the wall blend oddly with the tiles on the outside of the building across the street: if you sight out of one eye, your whole field of vision is one mass of Portuguese *azulejos*, the ones indoors and the ones across the street.

Bread and black olives arrive with the wine, and the Mediterranean atmosphere is complete. I am in Lisbon again, for business, for pleasure, tick the right box if you can find it.

II

I am in Lisbon because of my mother, who pervades everything here, and yet if you had asked her what connection she had with Portugal, she would have said, 'None at all.'

How shall I describe my mother? I've said that she was a music teacher, and that's how most people knew her. With her white hair and her distinguished manner, she was the picture of a music teacher and church organist. She had worked her way through college in the 20s, and by teaching in alternate years acquired a Bachelor of Music degree from Butler University in Indianapolis. She taught at schools in Indiana and Illinois, and was popular with the other teachers and pupils. In her later years she became a Quaker and was interested in New Testament studies, social problems and international relations. This description will give an impression of piety and rectitude, which is only part of the story. She was by no means a dull companion, and all through her life she attracted people who enjoyed being around her. She had a very merry sense of humour and laughed easily. She was quick to see the ridiculous side of things and liked funny stories. When I was grown up she still used to enclose cartoons from *The New Yorker* and *The Saturday Review* in her letters to me.

She was born in December 1902 to William and Grace Reed on a small farm near Avon, in Hendricks County in central Indiana. William was a farmer, blacksmith and skilled cabinet-maker. They had already lost two sons, twins born prematurely, and so Fern Lorraine Reed grew up an only child, living on various farms in Washington and Center Townships,* and in the town of Danville. Although she often saw her grandparents and several aunts and uncles, much of her childhood was lonely and she longed for siblings and playmates. (But her lonely childhood did not make her a shy adult. When I knew her she was gregarious and equal to any social situation.)

At eight Fern Reed came down with a streptococcus infection which almost killed her. ('Those were the days before sulpha drugs and penicillin,' I would be told in an aside when this story was being recounted.) For two years she was bed-ridden, gradually growing weaker and thinner. Two pus-filled abscesses the size of grapefruit formed at her right armpit and groin. The Reed side of the family saw the writing on the wall and began to prepare William for the inevitable death of his daughter. It must have been an agonising time for him; he had already made coffins for his two little sons. Grace Reed, however, was a Chambers, and they did not take things lying down. They generally had fiery tempers, loud voices, and little tact. In Grace these traits now took the form of a steely determination that her daughter would survive in spite of any weak-kneed doubts on the part of her in-laws. She had already lost two babies, and she was not going to lose this one, too. She faithfully beat up the eggs and whisky prescribed by the doctor. (Fern hated the taste of this concoction and would begin to cry when she heard the fork in the bowl. Finally Grace took the wretched stuff behind the barn to whip it up so that the nastiness of the medicine would at least be confined to the moment when it had to be drunk.)

What saved the situation turned out to be neither the Reed acceptance nor the Chambers determination and certainly not the whisky and eggs. It was a young doctor with a bright idea which now seems like only common sense. He suggested

* In the United States, a township is an administrative subdivision of a county.

lancing the abscesses at the armpit and groin. This surgery was not performed in a hospital or even in a doctor's office, but in the front yard of the Reeds' house on Mill Street in Danville. Fern was placed in a large chair and cushioned on pillows, and there, in the summer of 1912 in full view of the neighbours and any curious passers-by, the large sacs of pus were lanced. Fern began to get better almost immediately.

During her illness and convalescence her father helped her with her school work. He was good at arithmetic and passed his pleasure in numbers on to his daughter. All their lives my mother and her father enjoyed the sort of puzzle that begins, 'If John has 34 marbles and gives Bill twice as many as he gives Robert …'

I think that even as early as her convalescence she was already reading Sir Walter Scott. She loved the Waverley Novels, so much so that over 50 years later when she came to visit me in Scotland and I showed her Loch Katrine as though I had dug it myself, she exclaimed delightedly, 'Oh, Loch Katrine! The Lady of the Lake!' In fact, she knew more about Scottish topography than I, who had been living there for a year.

After she recovered from the streptococcus infection she made up for lost time. She learned to swim in the farm creek and at school played softball and basketball. Later she gave up ball games only because she was afraid of injuring her hands, as the piano was more important to her than sports. (That was the main difference between us: faced with this dilemma at sixteen, I would certainly have given up the piano in case it damaged my hands for basketball.)

At about this time something happened that was never satisfactorily explained. She woke up one Sunday morning unable to see clearly out of her right eye. Except for the periphery, everything was a grey cloud. She went to church and looked at the preacher out of first one eye and then the other and tried to blink the grey cloud away. Her eyesight remained impaired for the rest of her life, and although she always wore glasses, one lens was only plain glass ('window glass', she would call it). It had surprisingly little effect on her life, and only people in the family, a few ophthalmologists, and the Indiana Bureau of Motor Vehicles knew that for all practical purposes she was blind in one eye. Eye specialists would stare long and hard into her eye and call in their colleagues to take a look. The retina was clearly scarred in some way, but what had caused it? She somehow developed enough depth perception to play a good game of tennis and croquet, shoot baskets and hit softballs, be a good shot with a .22 rifle and drive anything with four wheels.

In 1919 she was president of the junior class. The following year she was voted 'best-natured student', as reported in the 1921 yearbook, of which she was editor. She graduated from Danville High School *cum laude* in the spring of 1921; it would have been *magna cum laude* if it hadn't been for her physics grade. ('We had to wire up electric bells and make them ring,' she used to say, with an expression indicating that this was an unreasonable thing to ask of anybody.) She went to the Metropolitan School of Music in Indianapolis the following year and began teaching with a temporary licence.

At some of those schools in the 20s she was the first music teacher they had ever seen. Prohibition was in full, if ineffectual, swing. Even in those out-of-the-way rural areas there were still speakeasies. Although Fern never drank herself (the eggs and whisky in her childhood had put her off alcohol for ever), she drove her less sober friends to and from roadhouses where bootleg liquor was sold. ('What!' I said on hearing this story, scandalised as only an adolescent can be. 'But there was nothing else to do in those little places,' she said, shrugging.)

Fern had learned to drive a car in 1921 and for the next 60 years she drove regularly and well. She used to say that in all those years she had never cost her insurance company a penny. She began to drive in the days when every make of car had a different gear system, before the standard shift was introduced. She learned partly by trial and error ('In those days you could learn to get out of a skid by practising on the highway. There wasn't much other traffic.'). By the time she taught me to drive on the country roads around Danville I couldn't have had a better teacher. I sometimes think that if she had been of a later generation she might have been a rally driver. I imagine her driving with a Land Rover team overland on terrible roads to the sort of place you need vaccinations for.

She was a good-looking young woman and dressed well. She made some of her clothes herself, including a winter coat. In old photographs her dark hair is corrugated with marcel waves. Sometimes she wears a fashionable cloche hat, and in full-length pictures smart long-waisted dresses and ropes of beads. She had a number of boyfriends during these years, and two or three fiancés, but she didn't marry until she was in her 30s. In her, and the century's, 20s an elderly janitor approached her one day after school and said haltingly, 'Miss Reed, I hope you'll take this the way an old man means it. An artist might not choose you for a model, but a sculptor sure would!' The shy sincerity of the old man amused and touched her, and years later she would tell the story and say that it was one of the nicest compliments she had ever received.

In 1923-24 she was at the University of Illinois at Champaign-Urbana, living at the Theta Upsilon sorority house. This would be just another of those hazy years of my mother's youth before I was born, but for one thing. From January to June 1924 she kept a diary. It is strange and touching to read your mother's thoughts when she is half your age and as yet unacquainted with your father. What a lively young woman she was! I think I would be charmed by this college girl even if she weren't my mother.

That renunciation of basketball was short-lived, because now she is the captain of the freshman girls' team. She swims and plays mah-jong and bridge and watches Mary Pickford and Harold Lloyd at the movies. She is enthralled by concerts by Heifitz and Marcel Dupré. She comes back to the sorority house at 1 a.m. after a sleighing party: 'They say that's the record for late hours here at the house and I got the proper bawling out.' She is taking various music courses (piano, cello, and harmony, at least), mathematics, rhetoric (which sounds like the freshman composition of a later day), history and Livy. Home for semester break in February, she reports: 'Mother and I shopped in Indianapolis today. We were just ready to catch the five o'clock car home when Uncle Let [Lester Reed, her father's younger brother] appeared and I talked him into driving us out and spending the night. We *both* drove the car home – I sat between him and Mother, guided, managed the gas and the brake – Uncle Let worked the clutch and spark – it was a *Ford Coupe*. We sang and had a good time all the way home.'

'Fun' and 'pep' are recurring words. Things are 'lots of fun' and the highest praise is 'lots of pep'. And the dances! Dances at fraternity houses, dances at country clubs, informal dances, formal dances, dances with trios, quartets, and orchestras! At a Cosmopolitan Club dance on the campus in April she says, 'Sandford and I did a fancy kick step out on the front porch, and Spencer and I did a dance between dances while Russell whistled *O Sole Mio*. Lots of fun.'

After one of my better semesters at Indiana University 40 years later, I made the Dean's List and asked Mother if she had ever been on the Dean's List. She thought for a moment and said she never knew the Dean *had* a list.

She couldn't afford to go back to the University of Illinois the next year. She sold hats at Wasson's in Indianapolis in the summer of 1924 while she looked for a teaching job. And there her diary ends and the vivid life returns to scrappy anecdotes and my vague, second-hand perspective on Fern's early days. But that college girl is still discernible one way or another for the rest of her life.

Still in the 20s, she was teaching grade school music and

high school English at a small school in northern Indiana. At the beginning of the school year she wrote home to her parents, 'The coach said, after our opening exercises this morning, "Well, I have a compliment for you. I never heard them make that much noise on the school song before." I almost said, "Big boy, makin' 'em sing is the best thing I am at." But I didn't.'

Back in Hendricks County a few years later, she had taken her chorus and an accompanist to a newly-built church in Brown Township for a festive official opening. The chorus had performed its number and Fern had then sat down in a front pew with the pianist, a plump young woman. In those days Fern used a baton for her choral directing, and now as the preacher began his oration, she absent-mindedly tapped it on the stack of hymnals beside her in the pew. The tip of the baton somehow got caught in a crack between the books and the other end slipped out of her hand so that the baton flipped end over end across the church, barely missing the startled preacher, who stopped in mid-sentence. Unbelievably, the baton then dropped neatly down the pipe of a marimba standing against the far wall.

The front few rows of the congregation began to chuckle and then laugh to such an extent that the people in the back, who had seen nothing, started to whisper among themselves, asking what had happened. Fern and the pianist tried to repress their own giggles, but the stout accompanist made the pew rock alarmingly. With the whole congregation either in fits of laughter or else wondering in increasingly loud murmurs what was going on, the preacher lost the thread of his remarks and, flustered, announced the final hymn. As a child I found a baton in a bookcase, brown bakelite with white ends, tapered toward the tip. I never once saw her use it; she always directed with her hands.

At most schools her duties as music teacher involved her in convocations and pep sessions before the games. The piano would be rolled out onto the gym floor and she would play the school song, often an adaptation of 'Illinois Loyalty' or the Indiana University alma mater, and then the more rousing 'fight song'. If stirring music was required when the team ran out onto the floor, either at the pep session or at the game that night, Fern would play a Souza march or 'On, Wisconsin' or perhaps a tune she had composed herself.

In 1936 in Chicago she married Lindol Lawson, the son of a Danville doctor. He was almost nine years younger than she was, but he seemed older than that. He was a charming and intelligent young man, a good dancer, and a would-be novelist. As a student at Central Normal College in Danville he had learned to fly an airplane, and a family snapshot shows him standing in an old-fashioned flier's rig-out beside a biplane. In Chicago he worked for a mail-order firm. He and Fern were deeply in love and very happy together. After they had been married for almost two years and had one child, something happened which was the watershed of Fern's life. After August 1938 her life was divided into Before the Accident and After the Accident.

'Chicago,' I think, sitting here in Lisbon 50 years later. How we are marked by places, by the cities where things happen. I hardly know the city of Chicago at all, but whatever public meaning it has, it is always the city where my parents lived and where my mother was hit not just by a car, but by two cars at the same time.

III

I walk past a hospital and encounter a number of people wearing casts on their arms or legs. Young men hobble along on crutches, and I wonder what sort of accidents they have had. The traffic in Lisbon is frightening. Sometimes it's hard to see the little green man giving you the right-of-way at pedestrian crossings because there are so many cars in the way.

One summer afternoon in Chicago Fern was crossing a street when two cars collided and slewed into her. She heard the screeching brakes and had just enough time to jump behind a sapling growing out of the sidewalk. It broke the impact but did not prevent her being thrown through the air and having both legs broken. As the inevitable group of excited passers-by collected and argued about what to do, Fern reached up from where she lay and tugged the hem of a man's suit jacket. Probably the most lucid person in the group, she told him (with that Reed calm and pragmatism!) where she lived and asked him to contact her landlady. The rest of this little *ad hoc* street-accident committee then decided to bundle her into an ordinary passenger car instead of waiting for an ambulance. The driver raced to the American Hospital, where he and a companion clasped their hands in a fireman's chair and carried her into the emergency department. She used to say that as they carried her she could feel the jagged splinters of her shattered thigh bone crunching together.

She was in shock for several days and was therefore not

given an anaesthetic when the broken right femur and left tibia were set. Several big strapping orderlies pulled mightily on her feet or lower legs. I always imagined them like a tug-of-war team straining to pull her legs straight, but I wonder if it could really have been like that.

When her parents arrived in Chicago, William Reed went to the street corner where Fern had been hit and found the remains of the little tree. He took a piece of the bark as a souvenir, and I found it years later in the bottom of his Seth Thomas mantle clock. On the back he had written neatly, 'Bark from the tree that saved Fern's life.'

She spent the rest of 1938 in traction, then a body cast. Lindol brought an electric fan to the hospital; Chicago is sweltering in August even without a body cast. She listened to the radio and followed the disturbing events in Europe. She read *Gone With the Wind* lying on her back and wove hot-dish mats on the little hand loom her father made for her. Once one of the specialists who came to examine her complained that there was no room on her bedside table for him to put down his bag of instruments. 'But I *live* here!' she told him.

Fern progressed from crutches to a leg brace and canes. It was another year or more before she could walk confidently across a room again without holding onto chairs and tables. She learned to walk normally, but she never enjoyed it and often had pains in her legs. I was born five years later, postponed because of the Accident and lucky to come on the scene at all.

When they moved back to Danville in 1939, Lindol began to study law at night and work in a law office in Indianapolis during the day. Fern taught music at Avon from 1940 to 1943. They lived with Lindol's parents: W.T. Lawson, 90 in 1939, a doctor and trustee of Central Normal College, and his third wife, Margaret, 20 years younger and a pillar of the Presbyterian Church and most of the local ladies' clubs. Lindol junior was looked after in this household and also that of his maternal grandparents, who still lived on a farm near Danville.

The suit for damages dragged on in Chicago. In 1941 Fern was awarded partial damages, but the case was complicated by the disappearance of the defendant. It was 10 years after the Accident that she was notified of the final hearing. Anxious to have the case closed at last, she took time off school, bought some new grey shoes, and flew to Chicago. Her old bone specialist, Dr Turner, once more described her broken femur and tibia, complete with X-rays, and her lawyer, Mr Whitney, extracted further damages from the insurance company.

While she was teaching choral music at Avon, the high school band director remarked that he could always tell which pupils had been Fern's: 'They're the *singin'est* kids I've ever seen!' he exclaimed. In 1941 Fern directed the Avon Boys' Chorus in 'The Riff Song' from *The Desert Song* in the annual All-County Musical and it brought the house down. At the rehearsal the singers themselves applauded their director, and at the Musical in the Central Normal gymnasium the applause was so thunderous that Fern stepped back onto the podium and did the chorus again as an encore. 'Part of it was the type piece that it is,' she recorded modestly in her diary.

At many of the schools where she taught, Fern gave piano lessons after school or during the lunch hour. She even gave piano lesson *before* school in 1942 when the nation set its clocks forward an hour for the war effort but the school at Avon opened at the same time, now 9 a.m. In the summer she gave lessons at the school every Tuesday. During most of the 1940s she also gave piano lessons at home on the baby grand. Sometimes she would hold a music book over the pupils' hands at the keyboard so that they couldn't look at them. She looked down at her own hands when she was playing, but she said that it was a bad habit. When they played a piece to her satisfaction she always stuck a pretty sticker on that page. She chose these stickers carefully; there were pumpkins for Hallowe'en, turkeys for Thanksgiving, hatchets for George

Washington's Birthday and stars of every colour. It all looked like great fun to me, and I was eager to learn to play the piano too and get colourful stickers, but it was harder than it looked.

As a child – in fact until I went abroad at 23 – I was constantly meeting old pupils of hers. They were everywhere. They would approach us in Ayres' tearoom in Indianapolis and say tentatively, 'Miss Reed?' They would come out to fill up the gas tank and exclaim, 'Why it's Mrs. Lawson, isn't it?' Balding men with wives and children would pull their families across the street to us and say, 'Aren't you Miss Reed? Jenny, this is my old music teacher!' The ones who had known her before her marriage would be gently corrected: 'I'm Mrs. Lawson now.' Fern invariably remembered them and what sort of voices they had had or whether they had been apt piano pupils. She would tell me of some pupil of 25 years before, 'She could read music like nobody's business!' Or she might shake her head regretfully and say, 'He was a nice boy, but he couldn't carry a tune in a bucket.'

By the time I knew Fern Lawson, her hair was mostly white; the Reeds all had prematurely white hair. After the Accident she had had to give up all her old sporty pastimes except for croquet, which she played in our cut-throat Midwestern way with gleeful ruthlessness. The first house I remember was a big white brick place on West Marion Street in Danville. In the east side yard we laid out a croquet court every summer under the persimmon tree. I can see her now, purposely choosing the last colour on the stake so that she could play off everyone else who went before her and be well on her way to the end stake before anyone else had a second turn. The wickets and stakes had to be taken up every week or two when the lawn was mowed, and later in the Fall there were too many persimmons on the ground to play croquet.

Our old brick house at the corner of West Marion and South Kentucky had been built in the 1840s. It was white with green shutters and was too solid and four-square to be called 'rambling', but it had all the charm, especially for a child, of a more literally rambling house. With its two overlapping run-arounds it was perfect for our rowdy games of cowboys-and-Indians. In the centre of the house was a long curving staircase with a walnut balustrade so precipitous that I didn't dare slide down more than the last few feet of it. The stairwell was papered from top to bottom with little repeating hunting scenes: clumps of trees, huntsmen in red coats on horseback and somewhere, presumably, a fox. There was a balcony over the front porch from which you could climb onto the roof, and another balcony over the glassed-in back porch. The only access to the back one was across the garage roof via an upstairs window. The summer Fern was told by a doctor to get more sunshine, she used to take her old towel with Roman stripes that she got in 1930 for the beach in Chicago and climb out onto the back balcony for an hour of undisturbed reading.

In 1947 Fern and Lindol were divorced. Anyone familiar with alcoholism will not need the details of Lindol's life, and anyone else would scarcely believe them. He had begun to drink heavily as a young man during Prohibition, and in spite of attempts to stop and long periods without alcohol, by about 1945 his drinking had become a serious problem. It interfered with his law practice, damaged his health and destroyed his marriage. Sober, he was a charming companion; drunk, he was impossible to live with. The sorrow with which Fern filed for the divorce contrasts poignantly with the joy with which they began their married life. She filed for the divorce in the spring and after a six-month separation it was made final in the Fall. There was no alternative. 'It is so extremely sad, but I *couldn't* go back into it,' she wrote in her diary on the day the divorce was granted, perhaps the saddest day of her life.

That year the only job she could find was 60 miles away in Middletown, where she and my brother took an apartment and she taught high school English. Just divorced, away from home and one of her children, and starting a new job where she knew no one, she nevertheless made such a striking impression that she was elected senior class co-sponsor in her second week at the school. She wrote in her diary, 'Elected co-sponsor of the Senior class today. Seniors elect sponsors first and it is quite an honor. Perhaps my white hair hasn't made an unfavorable first impression on the "teenagers" after all.'

I was too young to accompany them and stayed with my Reed grandparents, who had by now retired and moved to town. During the week I lived with them on North Indiana Street, and at weekends when my mother and brother came home we went to our house on West Marion. It was by no means empty during the week, because Danville was a college town and there was a post-war housing shortage. We rented rooms. I can still remember the names of 18 people who lived with us at various times before I was eight, and there must have been more. I recall sleeping in three different rooms downstairs; when the back bedroom was rented to two young women, we converted the dining-room into a bedroom and my grandfather constructed a temporary clothes closet out of one of the deep doorways.

This makeshift system of teaching in Middletown and coming back to Danville on most weekends mercifully lasted for only one year. By the next summer we were back together at the Old Brick House. On hot evenings we would go for a drive in the Buick for a breath of moving air. We would drive through nearby hamlets on country roads loud with the noise of locusts and grasshoppers. We would usually get ice cream or a Popsicle on the way and come back after dark. At Christmas and Thanksgiving and birthdays the Reeds would gather: we three and my grandparents and my grandfather's brother Lester (the merry driver of the Ford Coupe in 1924) and sister Millie. (My Lawson grandparents were both dead by now.) Later on Lester, a widower with two grown-up daughters, remarried and then we had Aunt Catherine, too.

We went to the Presbyterian Church, where Fern played

the organ. She had become a Presbyterian when she married into the Lawson family, although the Reeds were Baptists. After church we would sometimes walk home by way of the Rexall drugstore on the courthouse square and have a hot-fudge sundae. Fern was always very fond of ice cream, so much so that later when we were grown up my brother remarked that Mother was the only person he knew who ate ice cream *à la mode* [that is, topped with ice cream]. On most Sunday afternoons after we had read the funny papers, my brother and I went uptown to the movies. The movie house was on the other side of the courthouse square two blocks away. If it was a musical, Mother would sometimes come with us; she was very partial to Fred Astaire.

When we three went to the movies together, my brother and I would ask to move to the front, but Mother would always stay about three-quarters of the way back. We would scurry forward to the second or third row, where the screen glittered under the images, and white areas like Fred Astaire's spats and shirt-front were covered with tiny sequins. Sometimes I would turn around and look at the audience behind us. Scattered among the shadowy figures were pairs of bright reflections. I could always identify my mother instantly by the angle of her glasses because she held her head at a slightly different angle from anyone else. I never noticed this except at the movies. Was it because of her 'window glass'? It never occurred to me that she might have to compensate for her bad eye, because it never seemed to be a hindrance as far as anyone else was aware.

Fern was teaching fifth and sixth grades at New Winchester now. New Winchester was a crossroads with a few houses, but there was a school there because it was Section 16 of Marion Township, the one designated in all Indiana townships for the school whether there is a town nearby or not. She taught both grades in one big, well-lit room. One December her literal-minded fifth- and sixth-graders, with more birthday candles than tact, conscientiously stuck 48 of them into the top and sides of a cake for her.

It was in the following spring that she looked out of the windows along the west side of the room and watched the old barn, once used by pupils to stable their horses, come apart. A storm had been brewing, but the modern system of tornado warnings and alerts did not exist then. Now at New Winchester a tornado dipped down and took the barn roof with it. The roof rose in the air in front of Fern's startled gaze as she was dictating spelling words to her fifth grade. Still more or less in one piece, it began to roll end over end like a giant piece of tumbleweed down the big playground toward the football field. 'Children,' she said in the middle of the spelling test, 'come with me.' They all filed out into the hallway, where there were glass doors at each end. To avoid any possible flying glass, Fern led them down the north stairs to the girls' dressing room in the basement.

A few moments later my second-grade class was taken downstairs, too. The tornado proper had probably passed by then, but we stayed below ground during the ensuing thunderstorm. Two of the older girls began to sob hysterically because they suddenly remembered the Coatesville tornado, which had flattened a nearby town. To stop the hysteria from spreading, Mother led us in diverting songs. We sang, 'How in the heck can I wash my neck if it ain't a-gonna rain no more?' We sang nonsense songs and two-part rounds. She could direct massed choruses of good singers in Gounod or Sigmund Romberg; she could also amuse small apprehensive children in a school basement with some of the silliest songs ever devised. ('Now, this group sings, "Ham and eggs" and *you* sing, "Ham and eggs." Then the first group sings, "I like mine fried good and brown," and you sing, "I like mine fried upside down." Let's try that so far. Ready? "Ham and eggs, ham and eggs. I like mine fried good and brown, I like mine fried upside down." *Good*!') I never knew where she got them all. Looking back, I'm struck by the way she could be dictating spelling words one moment and averting panic the next. She knew as much about tornadoes as any other Midwesterner. She had seen what was left of Coatesville. Three years before, a tornado had brushed our house and uprooted a massive maple in the backyard. But she also knew that once you had taken shelter underground there wasn't much more you could do about it and you might as well enjoy yourself.

A group of any age couldn't help getting into the mood of the thing; she was enthusiastic and her directing was easy to follow. We came back upstairs still singing and giggling, and when we got back to our room our teacher tried to lead us in funny songs, but it didn't work at all and the mood was broken. We subsided into arithmetic and didn't find out about the barn until the bell rang and school was out.

Fern didn't spend much time in the summer lying in the sun, in spite of her doctor's orders. For one thing, the Reeds with their fair skin were not cut out for sunbathing, and for another thing, she was too busy working. Teachers needed second jobs if they were to be solvent all year round. She taught at a speech therapy school in Indianapolis and later she sold encyclopedias.

Sometimes during those years I would come bouncing into what I took to be an empty room and find my mother sitting in the dark smoking a cigarette. I was too young to be told or even to overhear anything about the financial problems or emotional upheavals, and I was much too young to be able to surmise them. There were conferences with her parents that went on into the night, and there were after-dinner discussions with her closest friends. There were long telephone conversations and sheets of paper covered with figures in her distinctive hand with the tails of the 7s and 9s below the line. I realised what these difficulties must have been only much later after I was grown up. At the time I hardly knew what personal problems she might have. She rarely mentioned them and she was never, so far as I can remember, irritable or short-tempered with me except when I deserved it. I think she dealt with everything the way she dealt with learning to walk again or filing for divorce or sitting out a tornado; I think she took a deep breath, decided on the best course of action and then methodically embarked on it. It looks to me, surveying her life from this vantage point, like a startling combination of the Chambers doggedness and the Reed calm.

Fern sold the Old Brick House and we went to live in Speedway on the western edge of Indianapolis for a few years in a bungalow with such small front and back yards that there was no room to play croquet. The only redeeming feature of the house was a wine-coloured ping-pong table in the basement left by the previous owners. My brother and I played on it a lot, and Fern would sometimes join us, using her only slightly modified tennis serve, which made us laugh.

I am struck now by her tolerance toward my pets. While we lived in Speedway I had numerous cats, a collie, and in the bedroom we shared, a parakeet, a terrapin and some goldfish. Sometimes one of the cats slept on my bed and if there was a litter of kittens I put them in an apple crate beside my bed. Occasionally I would find a fledgling and try unsuccessfully to keep it alive. Later (back in Danville in my teens) I even briefly had a couple of bats, and once I accidentally allowed a hummingbird to get loose in the dining-room. Fern resigned herself to my enthusiasm for animals, although the dog dug holes in the yard and the cats scratched the furniture.

One year a party of teachers from the Speedway Schools was taken around the nearby Indianapolis 500 racetrack and I went along. Fern drove around the two-and-a-half-mile oval, and the corners were so steeply banked that our Chevrolet tilted alarmingly. She would have enjoyed this, because she liked to drive cars, and practically any novelty was 'an interesting experience'. (I think that anything that was not actually an irredeemable disaster was 'an interesting experience', and this attitude undoubtedly accounted for much of her buoyancy and attractiveness. At various times in my youth 'an interesting experience' was made to cover lost tennis matches, disappointing marks on exams, and stitches in my scalp.)

When William Reed died it was like being hit in the solar plexus. Aunt Catherine phoned us at four in the morning, but it was too late. We got to the house a few minutes before the funeral director. Unaccustomed relatives arrived and a funeral had to be planned. I had been to funerals before because my grandparents' elderly friends would have them from time to time, but I had not considered the possibility of my own grandfather having one. Fern must have been devastated, but I do not remember any displays of grief beyond a quiet, numb sorrow. The Reeds were by no means cold or unemotional, but they seemed to have a built-in dignity made up of a natural calmness and practicality. We went to the undertaker's to choose a casket. Fern looked at them all carefully and listened to the undertaker's sales talk. Her grief took the form of a polished mahogany casket. 'Dad would have appreciated the quality,' she remarked sadly, stroking the wood.

Fern continued to teach, mostly in the grades now, and tried selling encyclopedias full-time. Life as a teacher was not all effortless fun and popularity with the children. She worked hard and there were extra-curricular obligations, especially PTA meetings. As a young teacher she had rehearsed her choruses and directed plays; she had drunk hurried cups of Sanka and eaten quick sandwiches between piano lessons or while overseeing dress rehearsals, but when I knew her she didn't like to go back out in the evening after a full day at school.

It was one of those summers when we were still in Speedway that Fern played the steam calliope. We had gone to a fish fry one Saturday afternoon at a Catholic church somewhere in Indianapolis, and as part of the entertainment a man was playing popular tunes on a calliope. Mother somehow began to talk to him – presumably during a break when he was down on the ground – and he invited her to try it out. I recall being surprised at her agility in climbing onto this combined bulldozer and pipe organ. I think she would have enjoyed putting it into gear and driving it around the block, but instead she tore into 'Stars and Stripes Forever', a favourite of hers when trying out any instrument with real noise potential. Standing down below looking up at my mother, I could sense the delight she took in operating the contraption and causing stirring music to issue from its pipes and valves.

I had learned before this that no row of black and white keys was ever going to give me any delight, except when it was played by somebody else. I had laboriously inched my way through the first two or three books in the tedious Thompson series. (Mother, on the other hand, always used the Schaum books, which were full of lively tunes and funny pictures.) Fern had engaged someone else to teach me piano, and every Thursday after school for a couple of years I went to the teacher's house with my piano book and my ill-prepared lesson. When I practised at home on the baby grand, my mother would hear my efforts from another part of the house. It must have been excruciating for her, but she was very philosophical about my lack of ability. My brother and I were required to take piano lessons for two years, after which we could drop them if we wanted to. This seemed a fair bargain, and she didn't mind when we both gave up as soon as we could. She had seen too many pushy parents ever to be one herself. I have heard her console herself with: 'Oh well, at least my children both have a good sense of rhythm.' She must have been thinking of our ping-pong, because there wasn't much evidence of it at the piano. Sometimes while I was practising she would call out from the kitchen or the bedroom, 'It's the black key *next* to that one,' and sure enough, when I worked it out she would be right. I never resented this correction; I knew I needed all the help I could get, but it was an odd sensation to be corrected from a distance by someone who wasn't even looking at the music.

After she died I thought of the skill and knowledge that was dying with her. I looked at her hands and thought how she struck the right piano keys effortlessly; how the left hand plucked chords to flesh out the design of the right hand; how she sometimes felt among the keys for the right note to start on. She read the blobs and strings on paper as easily as I read foreign words, but at least a foreign language has *words*. (She thought a course I took one year in 19th century Spanish literature sounded comically esoteric, but this was the woman who once took an entire course in piano pedalling. And what about Livy in 1924?) She could no doubt have picked up a Portuguese guitar, strummed it, tried out a few things, listened to the way it was tuned, made some little discoveries without being told, and played a melody. That, I realise with a start, is the way I read a Portuguese newspaper.

IV

The paving stones in Lisbon are mesmerising. The overall design seems to cover acres, but it is made up of small square setts put in place meticulously one by one. From north to south? From the centre outward? And so the pattern is built up, a pattern you can walk across, a pattern you can see from the air.

The pattern of Fern's life changed radically when, in her mid-50s, she retired from teaching and married her second husband, Harry Hadley. Harry had a degree in chemistry from the University of Illinois, but as a young man he had discovered that farming was both more enjoyable and more profitable than working in a laboratory. He had a big farm nine miles from Danville in Marion Township, and now we – my mother and I, as my brother was married by this time – went there to live.

In all her working life Fern had never been able to spend much time cooking or housekeeping – what she now called 'homemaking'. She revelled in new recipes and with Harry's encouragement redecorated the house. We had honey in the comb from the beehives, fresh eggs from the Leghorns, and a constant supply of Jersey cream. A freezer man called every few weeks and we bought frozen food in bulk, including gallons of ice cream and sherbet. ('Have some ice cream, Fernie!' she would say, scooping vanilla ice cream into a chili bowl.) Fern joined a few local clubs of other farm women and would do her share of entertaining them with luncheons or coffee parties. Now and then they would get people to speak or show slides. She worked diligently at her bridge, and she and Harry, who was a good bridge player, took part in continual rounds of bridge parties and charity tournaments. However, after a few years the novelty of this style of life began to pall. She needed something challenging, and it was at about this time that she and Harry joined the Society of Friends. From then until the end of her life she became increasingly involved in Quaker work.

Harry didn't like to drive and hadn't travelled much, but now with Fern to drive they began to go off on long tours of the western States and Canada. I would get postcards at college from Mexican border towns, the Canadian Rockies, Yosemite and other national parks, and picturesque lakeside hotels. There was plenty of room in the big Ford, and they would put a set of *Compton's*, the encyclopedia Fern used to sell, in the back seat to answer any questions that might come to them along the way. They went to Pike's Peak, where the usual custom is to leave one's car at the base of the mountain and take a special bus to the top. This practice is, however, optional, and Fern decided to drive to the top, to the stupefied amazement of the filling station attendant at the bottom of the mountain. (He needn't have been so amazed. I could have told him that it was going to be 'an interesting experience'.)

On another trip in the West she drove through an icy pass in the mountains and enquired at the next town about the condition of the roads farther along. When the man at the filling station discovered how she had arrived in the town, he said, 'Hell, Lady, if you've come through that pass, it don't matter what road you take!' I imagine filling stations throughout the West with stunned and wide-eyed attendants dumbly holding a gas nozzle in one hand and scratching their head with the other and watching the receding Ford (some years it was a Buick) with the white-haired lady at the wheel. In the Sierra Madre in Mexico the power steering had failed and driving down out of the mountains had been physically difficult. She drove in Mexico City and Los Angeles and Ottawa; they were in Seattle for the World's Fair.

On one of their jaunts to the West, they went through Manitou Springs, Colorado, where Lindol and his second wife were living. Out of curiosity to see his house, Fern and Harry drove slowly down the street and past the residence, only to discover that the street was a dead end and they had to turn around and drive back. As they did this, Lindol came out, saw that the car had Indiana licence plates, recognised Fern, and invited them in. (Now that I think of it, the Lawsons had a pretty creditable line in *sang-froid*, too.) Fern had not seen Lindol for 20 years, but what could have been deeply embarrassing turned into a fairly pleasant visit. (An English friend, hearing this story, asked, 'Did he offer them a glass of sherry?' 'No,' I said, 'I think not.')

She went to Quaker conferences all over the Midwest and East Coast. She went to the Friends Committee on National Legislation in Washington and to William Penn House in New York, where Quakers work for behind-the-scenes reconciliation among delegates to the United Nations. She attended a Friends' World Conference in North Carolina and later when I was living in Britain she visited Quaker meetings all over Europe.

Harry Hadley was 14 years older than Fern and his health began to fail. His emphysema got worse and he sometimes had to be rushed to the hospital and put in an oxygen tent until his condition stabilised. For several years Fern lived under the strain of looking after him and dealing with his moods and depressions. He died in 1975, coincidentally the same year that Lindol died. She stayed on at the Hadley farm for a few years and then moved to Plainfield, where she had an apartment at Quaker Village, a retirement complex.

She was in her 70s now and walking was increasingly difficult. She took some exercise every day, but her right hip joint was always painful. Not only had it been damaged in the Accident, but it had probably not developed properly because of the streptococcus infection. But in her big Ford LTD she could be as mobile as anyone else, and she still drove it, often full of other Quaker women, to Washington and New York, stopping for the night along the Pennsylvania Turnpike or elsewhere in the Appalachians. Leaving her car at home, she went around the world. Now instead of getting postcards from Yosemite and Lake Louise, I heard from Kyoto and Kathmandu. She stopped off in London to see me and brought me a souvenir of Bali. She had visited an old college friend of mine in Bangkok and brought me a little memento from her. She had seen the Taj Mahal and the Acropolis. The Middle East had been 'an interesting experience'. The hotel in Teheran had tried to cancel their reservations, but the tour guide had stuck to her guns and threatened never to use that hotel again, whereupon the rooms were all available after all. Israel was thrilling; she had seen the Mount of Olives and the Sea of Galilee. Jerusalem was unbelievably crowded: 'It was like the State Fair on Band Day!' she told me. (I pictured for a moment Indiana high school bands marching through the Holy Land, but I couldn't keep it up for long.)

Her modest apartment in Plainfield was beautifully furnished, so that people who were thinking of moving to Quaker Village were brought to Fern's apartment to see what the possibilities were. She wanted two telephones, but when she found that it would cost very little extra to have more, she got four and put them in every room including the bathroom. (I can imagine her costing it out, jotting down figures on a scrap of paper, the 7s and 9s ending firmly below the line.)

Similarly, there were three television sets. She enjoyed her possessions, as she enjoyed the rest of life. She liked gadgets. There had been no electricity at the Reed farm until 1935 and she had ironed by the light of a kerosene lamp with a flatiron heated on the coal stove. She enjoyed the trappings of modern life and felt no nostalgia about the past. ('"The Good Old Days",' she used to say, 'ha!') She had her telephones and televisions because they were easily available, but she could have lived without them. She was by no means an acquisitive person; 'Possessions,' she would say with a dismissive gesture, 'they're only possessions.'

Once we were talking about a cantankerous old lady we knew. Fern had known her as a younger woman, and her character had not changed as she had grown older, but had only become more noticeable. 'If you want to be a nice old lady,' Mother told me, 'you have to start practising early.' She didn't mean this to apply to herself, but she *was* a nice old lady, and she *had* put in a lot of practice. She firmly believed in the two New Testament commandments: 'Love God and love one another,' and she tried, usually successfully, to maintain good relations even with such unpromising material as her divorced son's ex-wife's second husband and the relatives of her own second husband's first wife.

At the end of her life her height had shrunk by two inches to 5'4", yet everyone remembered her as a tall woman. In her years of appearing in public and in front of classes, she had dressed with great care and had left an impression of taste and style. ('I remember your mother sitting there at the piano. She always dressed so well! I remember she used to wear some amber beads ...') From her early 30s her hair had gradually turned white, and it was so striking that perfect strangers would come up to her in Indianapolis department stores and ask where she had her hair done. As an older woman she knew exactly where she wanted her hemline, and she had a succession of dressmakers who made or altered clothes for her when she didn't have time to do it herself. She watched her weight carefully and rationed the ice cream (which was often ice milk anyway) and the pecan pie.

For all her dignity and religious conviction, I associate her with jokes, too. There was a strong streak of whimsy in all the Reeds, or perhaps the presence of a small child in their midst brought it out. My grandfather nearly always referred to New Winchester as 'New Chin-whiskers', at least in my hearing. (It occurs to me now that they may not have always been quite so whimsical among themselves.) Once I had a pair of pyjamas with a design of small red, blue, yellow and green umbrellas all over them. 'Now,' said my grandfather seriously, 'you can sleep out of doors in the rain.'

When I was little, my mother would try to encourage me to go to bed by clapping her hands and saying, 'It's time to hick-hike-hoke off to bed now!' This was evidently one of her nonsense phrases; I supposed the words were variations on 'hike' – 'it's time to hike off to bed'. I suddenly realised where they came from some years later when I was memorising the 30 forms of the Latin demonstrative adjective – *hic, haec, hoc* in the nominative singular.

The first joke I ever heard in my life my mother told me when I was about four. It was about a lady who is surprised to find a rabbit sitting in her refrigerator. 'Why, Bunny Rabbit!' she exclaims, 'What are you doing in my refrigerator?'

'What kind of refrigerator is this?' asks the rabbit.

'A Westinghouse,' says the lady, puzzled.

'Well,' explains the rabbit, 'I'm westing.'

When the joke was explained to me, I found it very funny and wanted to hear it over and over. I liked the voices Fern used for the surprised housewife and the relaxed rabbit. As we had a Westinghouse, I half thought it might really happen sometime.

Another joke that she relished (and told me long after the rabbit joke) concerned a woman who learns from her doctor that she is pregnant. When she protests tearfully that she can't possibly go through with it again, he points out that although her other children are almost grown up, her earlier pregnancies have been normal with no complications. She says, 'It's not *that*, doctor, it's the PTA meetings!' When something was really funny, Fern would have to take her glasses off and wipe her eyes.

Doubly widowed and now installed in Plainfield, she told me that she was looking forward to starting a new phase in her life. She had season tickets to two new theatres in

Indianapolis and took university extension classes in literature and politics. She joined the Book-of-the-Month Club again after a lapse of 40 years. She bought the latest model electronic sewing machine and signed up for a course of lessons on how to use it and how to sew the new stretch fabrics.

Her husbands had both been Republicans. The Reeds, however, were staunch Democrats, and in the perilous 1930s Fern had actually lost her job at Danville High School because the new trustee had decided to replace her with a Republican. (It wasn't so much that *she* was a Democrat, but her father had run for county office and was active in the local party.) It was never very advisable to be known as a Democrat in Hendricks County if you wanted your business to prosper; your customers would be mostly other Democrats, and there weren't many. Now, however, with nothing to lose, Fern came out as a Democrat and worked for a Democratic congressional candidate. She contributed to campaign funds and attended Jefferson Day dinners ('If only Dad could be here now!' she wrote me.)

On her 78th birthday she was busy planning another trip. 'I'm not just going to sit around and do fancy work, you know,' she told me. 'I have plans! I have things to do!'

V

It was here in Lisbon that I last saw my mother alive. We were staying at the Hotel Valverde then, up near the Pombal monument and just off the Avenida da Liberdade. Seven years ago we saw Lisbon with our hotel as the focal point, the place we left from and came back to. We walked down the Avenida and back up. Now I am down at the other end of the Avenida and the city looks entirely different.

I walk through the bustling Rossio, the square where the National Theatre is and where the Palace of the Inquisition used to be. It was an open square before the earthquake and was left an open square when the rest of the city was rebuilt. The guidebook says of it, 'It has a lively gayful atmosphere, with its cafés and esplanades always crowded with people.' Even at this time of year it is pretty gayful and there are a good many tourists.

The next square is the Praça dos Restauradores, and then the Avenida proper starts. There are little access streets at each side, then the esplanades, like long narrow parks, with benches at intervals along the mosaic pavement, numerous palm trees, and even a stream with swans along one stretch. Bare deciduous trees are dotted among the palms – what I have learned to call plane trees but my mother would have recognised as sycamores. Between the two esplanades are the lanes of traffic of the Avenida roaring up and down the long slope between Restauradores and the Praça Marquês de Pombal. There are restaurants on the esplanades with white tables and chairs under the trees. You can eat either outside or inside, where you can watch the traffic go by at a muffling distance.

I am only out for a stroll; I do not really intend to go to the Hotel Valverde; but almost as though someone else is in charge of my feet, I turn down a side street which takes me to Rua Rodrigues Sampaio. There are shops and a medical practice and then I come to the Hotel Valverde, exactly as I remember it. There is an empty little restaurant attached and a small lobby. The bar and television lounge are out of sight around a corner, and the two elevators are hidden by an opaque glass partition, but I know exactly where they are. The Hotel Valverde was the idea of Gladys, my mother's travel agent in Indianapolis. The front window is covered with stickers for credit cards and tour companies of many nationalities and several car rental firms. Across the street is the back of the *Diário de Notícias* building, and there are some small vans and cars with the name of the newspaper written on the side. I walk in the direction we used to, up to the end of the street and out onto the Avenida da Liberdade where the Rotunda Metro station is. Everything looks familiar and it seems to me that I can even recognise the palm trees. Our footprints from seven years ago are here on this mosaic pavement if only I had magic glasses to see them.

Naturally, Fern did not do all this walking. When we came here we rented a wheelchair from a company that supplies hospital and home nursing equipment. With the wheelchair all three of us could go for quite strenuous hikes through the city. On the whole, Lisbon is not a good place for a person with any kind of disability. Many of the streets are very steep, and many of them are simply flights of steps. You could fall down in one neighbourhood and finally come to rest in a quite different one. Still, we covered the main thoroughfares and even got up to the Castle.

The stooped figures in black shuffling along the narrow sidewalks make me think of Fern because they are so unlike her. Seven years ago she walked here, and she sometimes wore black, but well-cut, fashionable black with a little good jewelry. She liked good patent leather shoes and handbags. Her white hair was a snowy, well-cared-for white. Sometimes to make a fuller effect (for her hair was thinning on top) she wore a hairpiece. I feel a pang for the old ladies I see because she might have been like that if the circumstances of her life had been different or if she had lived longer. The pang I feel is partly a fear of what might have been or even, in my own case, what might yet be.

We used to sit in the little restaurant attached to the hotel and have our evening meal. Whatever exactly we talked about, I remember pleasant meals with stimulating conversation. The little restaurant was very plain, but the food was good. The pottery salt and pepper shakers were hand made, and one evening Mother drew our attention to them. She picked up first one and then the other and turned them around in her hands, examining them carefully. 'Look,' she said, 'they're hand-made.'

The monument to the Marquês de Pombal near the hotel was our main landmark. Pombal was the principal minister of Portugal during the reign of King José in the third quarter of the 18th century. He was a man of great energy and practicality in a period when the general tone of life in Portugal was one of lethargy and religious excess. Later in his term of office, Pombal became a tyrant, but at the beginning of his power his great achievement was to rebuild Lisbon after the earthquake in 1755. King José and his court were in panic. Most of the inhabitants of the capital were either dead, injured or homeless, and the destruction was on such a scale that the King didn't know where to begin. 'What is to be done?' he is supposed to have asked his minister. And Pombal replied with an admirable briskness: 'Sire, bury the dead and feed the living.'

His presence of mind in the aftermath of the earthquake conferred power on him for the rest of King José's reign, another 22 years. Today his monument at the top of the

Avenida da Liberdade where the Edward VII Park begins is encircled by four lanes of traffic, the most congested spot in Portugal. On the paving in front of the monument is an intricate mosaic design of a sailing ship on some stylised waves, and below that is a crown. There is a border of hedge-enclosed grass, more paving, then steps up to the base of the column. From the ground it is hard to make out the details of the figure at the top. It is a man in 18th-century dress and wig with a lion at his side. As so many such statesmen are shown mounted on horseback, perhaps the sculptor thought some animal or other was necessary. There are other groups of figures around the base of the column and medallions with busts in relief near the top. Even when not atop a pillar, Pombal was an impressive man. He was six feet tall and towered above the other men of his time, including King José.

There are glassy international hotels here at the top end of the Avenida da Liberdade and airline offices and big modern banks. The newspaper building, with pages from the current issue displayed behind glass, takes up most of the block. Taxis are everywhere, with their distinctive black bodies and green tops. It is a bustling, prosperous-looking city, post-earthquake and post-Salazar.

Seven years ago we didn't spend all our time in Lisbon. We met here, spent a few days, and then went off in a rented Citroën through southern Portugal and Andalusia. We came back through Córdoba and Badajoz into Portugal and on to Lisbon again, where we spent a few more days. The trip was Fern's idea. She had travelled widely, alone or with a tour group, but now she needed a bit more help (like that wheelchair) than an ordinary tour guide could give. We had travelled together in Europe – in France, Germany, Austria, and of course Great Britain. We went by car, and my husband and I did all the driving. I could understand why she didn't want to drive in Britain on the left side of the road and the right side of the car, but when we toured on the Continent together and she still showed no interest in driving, I suddenly realised with a shock that she was getting old.

I have come better prepared this time. I have a better guidebook, and before I left London I read about Lisbon and Portugal. I want to hear some fado music sometime. The guidebook gives the impression that fado is an acquired taste. It is the principal folk music of Portugal and is apparently a mournful wail for lost love and things generally going wrong. Fado is often about being unhappy, deserted by one's lover, or ignored by the man one loves. It sounds thoroughly depressing, a nervous breakdown scored for voice and guitar. I gather that only the Portuguese have the necessary soul and innate melancholy to appreciate it.

I find a shop that sells tape cassettes and I look through their collection of fado. I see tapes of Amália Rodrigues everywhere; she seems to be *the* exponent of the art. (Later I discover that she no longer sings, but has become a kind of legend, and her black shawl and guitar are now in the city museum.) I buy a tape more or less at random and play it on my walkman. The guidebook writer was being unnecessarily alarmist. If fado is an acquired taste, it takes a matter of seconds to acquire it.

Fado isn't always mournful. Sometimes it is a celebration of a certain province or town, especially Lisbon, but it can mean merely a song for a solo singer. Sometimes it concerns one's family, especially one's mother. Among the cassette tapes I find 'A Mother's Love', 'My Mother's Shawl', and 'A Fado For My Mother'. Armando Leça, in a book on Portuguese music, tries to explain the essence of fado. Lisbon, he says, is 'the nursery of the fado' and particularly the Alfama, where the atmosphere and surroundings are conducive to fado singing. It should be sung late at night in smoky taverns; away from its proper sphere, fado becomes 'unadaptable'. 'One should always be able to see the sea from the fisherman's house,' Leça says. Alberto Pimental, writing at the turn of the century, says that although fado is imitated in Coimbra in the North, it is not properly understood there and cannot really be transplanted. It is 'a hot-house plant that seems to weep for its native climate – the climate of disreputable quarters and dubious streets.' *The New Grove Dictionary of Music and Musicians* puts it more succinctly and less romantically, but the definition is essentially the same: 'the typical urban vocal music of cafés, cabarets and night clubs.'

Pimental quotes an earlier Spanish writer, who declares, 'The Fado requires absolute silence, mysterious shadow and a certain amount of sadness in the heart.' Most writers agree that the word *fado* derives from the Latin *fatum*, meaning 'fate', and fatalism hovers over the older melancholy fados.

The Portuguese are said to have a streak of melancholy and nostalgic longing in their character. The Portuguese word for this is *saudade*. Alberto Pimental says, 'We pride ourselves on possessing the word *saudade*, which expresses better than any other word in foreign languages the ache of absence.' My dictionary translates *saudade* as 'regret', 'sorrow', 'longing' or 'homesickness'. The expression that means 'remember me to him' is literally 'give him my *saudades*'. *Nostalgia* is a separate word, although it would seem to overlap with *saudade*. Fado, then, is the expression of this very Portuguese ache, although to my innocent ear it sounds equally French (think of Edith Piaf) or even American (Bessie Smith, for one).

The rounded Portuguese guitar can sound like a mandolin or a zither; it ripples and swirls behind the singer as she sings about her unhappy life. In Lisbon the *fadista* is usually a woman, ideally one past the first flush of youth who looks as though she has something convincing to sing about. Someone under 35 is unlikely to have made the requisite hash of her life yet. The singer, I gather, should be an alto with a throaty lower range. In her 40s or 50s, she has supposedly experienced ups and downs, especially downs, and has the maturity to reflect on them. Sometimes the guitar is played by itself with a beautiful, haunting effect. I soon accumulate several more fado tapes.

It is nearly Carnival time in Lisbon. There are odd bits of street theatre and here and there confetti on the sidewalk and ribbons of streamers. In a side street I find a little marching band of a dozen young men and some hangers-on. They are dressed in costumes, and although no one around them seems to be doing anything festive, they are a mini-carnival all by themselves. The saxophonist is dressed like a baby in diapers and a frilly bonnet. One of their hangers-on is throwing streamers over the little band and some bystanders. A drummer brings up the rear beating a cadence when the others are not playing.

The likelihood of Carnival crowds reminds me to hang on to my shoulder bag. I have heard that there is a lot of bag-snatching in Lisbon. A Canadian I have met here has warned me that there have been cases of motorbike pillion passengers grabbing bags from pedestrians, as in Rome. I resolve to be careful, but I wonder if Lisbon can be any more dangerous than London.

On a winter evening in central London the smell of hot chestnuts roasting over a charcoal brazier is as much a part of that season of the year as the early darkness and the damp chill of the air. It is strange to smell chestnuts here in Lisbon on a sunny, mild afternoon. They are roasted over a charcoal fire, and the breeze carries the smoke many yards down the street. The little oven in the street stalls looks like something that hasn't changed since Roman times. The bottom part holds the charcoal and is shaped like a cone, narrow at the base. On top of this sits another cone, narrow at the top, which is open to let the smoke out. The woman selling chestnuts in the Rua do Carmo puts a pound or two of chestnuts and a handful of coarse salt in this top cone. She sells them in a twist of paper for 100 escudos (about 40 pence). She expertly rips out a page from a volume of the Lisbon *Yellow Pages* she keeps on her table, makes a cone of it, and puts a big handful of nuts in it before folding the top neatly. The nuts are coated with a fine layer of grey ash from the charcoal and taste faintly of that and salt. They are delicious when I get used to eating them on a sunny, spring-like afternoon.

I walk up the steep Rua Sacramento to the Largo do Carmo to look at the old Carmo Convent, which was destroyed in the earthquake of 1755. It is still in ruins, but what was once the apse of this 14th-century Gothic church is intact, and that part serves as a museum of archaeology. In 1755 Lisbon was full of churches and on the morning of All Saints Day they were all packed with worshippers. People watching from boats in the harbour said that the city rippled like a field of grain as the earthquake shook the buildings. This church, then, high up above the Rua do Carmo, shook like grass in the wind before the roof fell in, killing the worshippers. Now the arches remain like hoops of a barrel, and the side aisles are paved walkways through a grassy little park. The arches are part of the Lisbon skyline, and in the evening they glow pink in the setting sun.

In the evening at the hotel I glean what I can from the *Diário de Notícias*. I even read comments about television programmes, ads for household appliances, the sports headlines and the obituaries. The latter are much more detailed than funeral announcements in English-language newspapers. They are mixed in with the job ads, but are unmistakable with the black crosses surrounded by white space. Below the cross in large type is the name of the deceased and often a photograph. A paragraph in small type tells where and when the Requiem Mass is to be and who the survivors are. Some of the people in the photographs look very young, as though they should be in some other part of the paper in a story about a new mayor in the provinces. Are these old photographs or did these people die young? I can't help wondering about their lives and the lives of the people they have left behind. Each little notice in the paper is a family crisis and a private disaster.

VI

Children seem to be the main beneficiaries of Carnival. Several days before Shrove Tuesday it is common to see small children dressed up in costumes, usually walking along with their parents, not in costume. Little girls of seven or eight wear medieval-lady confections of fluffy skirts and conical headdresses. Similar outfits minus the headdress suggest pink fairies. The clear favourite among little boys is a sort of Zorro suit. They wear cowboy hats and capes and a mask over their eyes. The outfits seem to have been bought somewhere, but some of them are home-made. These children seem to be on some plane of reality different from the rest of us. They are Zorro, a medieval lady, an Indian chief, a nurse, all romping along beside their staid, civilian parents. As I have never celebrated Carnival, it seems to me a curiously extravagant fling just to observe the beginning of Lent: the end of meat-eating and living it up, the beginning of penance and privation. Whatever the rationale behind it, it does lend jollity and colour to the street scene and ordinary life.

Seven years ago in Lisbon my husband and I needed a relief from ordinary life. We went to a Woody Allen film. I found it witty and entertaining, but I fell asleep before it was over.

The last evening before we were to leave Lisbon, we three ate in the restaurant of the Hotel Valverde and had a pleasant evening together. After I had packed and gone to bed, the telephone beside the bed rang. To my surprise it was Mother in the next room asking me to come. When I entered her room, wondering what she wanted, she told me she thought she was having a heart attack. She spoke so calmly and matter-of-factly that it took a moment for the meaning to register. She lay quietly on the bed ('Are you in pain?' 'No.') and I telephoned the hotel desk and asked for a doctor. Then I phoned again and asked for an ambulance. The doctor and the ambulance arrived at about the same time. The ambulance crew came up to the fifth floor in one elevator and the doctor in the other. The ambulance crew bundled her onto a stretcher, rushed back to the elevator, upended the stretcher to get it in, and shot back down to the lobby. My husband and I and the doctor took the other elevator, like a madcap chase sequence in a movie.

At the hospital the doctor on duty was chatting with the nurses when we rushed in with the stretcher. He pronounced her dead and then they wanted to take the body away. I stalled for time. We had all had dinner together only a few hours ago, and now she didn't exist any more. She had died before they got to the hotel. While the doctor was dressing and the ambulance men were starting their engine, her heart stopped. There had been three of us and now there were only two. I didn't want her to disappear so quickly. 'Wait,' I said. 'Just a moment.' They seemed impatient to take the body away. But what's the hurry? It can't be that urgent. 'Just a little time, please.' I want to look at her. She looks just unconscious. 'Wait a minute,' I say. 'Please wait.' This must be what wakes are for: to get used to someone you know turning into a dead body.

I have the idea that if I take her hairpiece off I can stall for more time. Her hair is piled up and I begin to take out the white bobby pins. It is a flimsy ploy, but it is the only thing I can think of. Why are they being so officious anyway? They will see what I'm doing and give me a little more time. Perhaps they will believe that this is something that needs to be done. I have no sense that this is a corpse or an object of disgust. This was so recently my mother that it still is my mother. I have taken out a dozen bobby pins when I realise that she isn't wearing a hairpiece after all. Now they will think that I have some peculiar attachment to bobby pins.

Finally there is no way to stall any more, and I let them take her away. I feel a sense of horror and disbelief. It's two in the morning and we are in the emergency department of this Portuguese hospital. It's a Monday night and business is a little slow. They don't seem to have much to do, except whisk bodies away before you're ready. There are no other ambulances. Our ambulance men have all gone away now. They've finished their job here. Perhaps they have had to rush off on another emergency.

The doctor – ours from the hotel – is a cardiologist. He takes me to a part of the hospital where there is a woman with a typewriter. She sits in a little office, even now at 2 a.m. She types records and statistics. The doctor asks me how old my mother was, when she was born. He wants her full name, too. He tells these words to the woman at the typewriter and she types them. Does she do this all night? My mother is going to be a part of the Portuguese vital statistics for this year. The cardiologist says it was a cardiac infarction. I have not heard of an infarction before, and he tells me what it means. (It was a coronary occlusion in my grandfather's day. I suppose they're the same. Same effect, anyway.) He speaks English and is very helpful. He came in his car, behind the ambulance. I came in the ambulance, lurching and bouncing through the streets with the siren wailing, my arm across my mother's body to steady her on the stretcher. That was only a few minutes ago. He says he will take us back to the hotel. There is nothing else to do but go back to the hotel. There is no reason to stay here any longer. There's no reason to go back to the hotel either, but we don't belong in this hospital, so we will go back to the hotel.

At the Hotel Valverde the man at the desk is very sorry and offers his sympathy. We go up to the fifth floor in the elevator. The cardiologist writes out a death certificate in Portuguese and another one in English. He offers to give me a sedative, but I don't want a sedative. I am sedate enough, but my mother is dead. She's still in that hospital. I had to leave her there.

What is to be done? We try to be practical, like Pombal. It's still evening in Indiana, so I telephone Quaker Village. I identify myself and say, 'My mother has just died.' Out of all the words I have uttered in my talkative life, I have never pronounced these five common words in this order before. The people at the Quaker Village are stunned at hearing what I tell them. It is all new to them. I have had two hours to think about it, but I am as stunned as they are. We talk for a few minutes, and they remind me about the bequeathal form. They were going to pick her up at the Indianapolis airport tomorrow. When daylight comes we will have to cancel her airline ticket and register her death with the American Embassy. I know that this unreality will pass and then the grief will hit. I haven't begun to cry yet. It will happen later. It is a delayed reaction. It is like certain kinds of wound that don't hurt at first, but only later.

The next morning we eat breakfast in the hotel restaurant. The events in the night have changed everything. The waiter brings us a boiled egg and some bread and a pot of tea. I'm not hungry but I try to eat some of the egg. The salt shaker, oh, the salt shaker. The hand-made pottery salt shaker. I can't see anything because of the tears. I keep wiping them away with the table napkin. We must go out. We must do things.

We go to a bank and then out onto the Avenida da Liberdade to the airline office, where they cancel the ticket and refund the cost of it. We go to the American Embassy, which is within walking distance. We explain what has happened and show them the certificates our cardiologist has given us, one copy in Portuguese and one in English. I explain that my mother wanted her body given to science when she died. She had planned to donate it to Indiana

University, but on the back of her bequeathal form she had added a codicil saying that if she died away from home her body should go to the nearest medical school. They stamp CANCELLED on her passport and write 'deceased' under the stamp and hand it back to me. I keep having to stop and take out a kleenex. My face is wet with tears and I have to blow my nose. One kleenex doesn't last long.

They say that they will contact a medical school, the one at the New University of Lisbon, and arrange for the body to be taken there. I must go there and sign a paper. The Embassy makes an appointment for me with the medical school. I am to see a Dr Fernandes, who teaches anatomy. The appointment isn't until the afternoon and we try to keep busy until then.

Dr Fernandes is in his 20s and seems grateful for this unexpected gift. He teaches anatomy with an enthusiasm I cannot share. He needs a statement from me saying that I am next of kin and I donate the body. I offer to type it out for him. I go into an office and sit at a typewriter. The keyboard is different on a Portuguese typewriter, and I have to correct two mistakes in the first word. This time yesterday we were happy and everything was fine, and now I am giving this medical school my mother's body. The typewriter goes out of focus with tears again and I have to stop.

Mealtimes are terrible. I try to eat, but can't. The food looks and tastes awful. I don't want to put it in my mouth. Even when I chew it up I can barely swallow it. When we stop doing things and having places to go, the full horror of the situation comes over me like handling nettles with gloves on and then taking off the gloves and handling the nettles without them. No, what it's like is a very painful kind of hay fever, where your eyes run constantly and you have to carry a box of kleenex everywhere and you're past caring what passers-by think. The empty, agonising evening stretches ahead of us, hours long. What can we do? We decide to go to a movie.

In the hotel room I lie on the bed, letting my eyes run. There is a knock at the door and it is a little group of three or four hotel maids. They say they are very sorry about the *senhora*, they are sorry for me. It is very nice of them to come; I thank them. The news is all over the hotel, of course. The night staff told the day staff. The man on the desk who had to phone for the doctor and an ambulance would have been in great demand. ('You'll never guess what happened here last night!') The maids would have known immediately who the desk man meant: the white-haired foreign lady with the nice smile who always greeted them in the hall and thanked them if they held the elevator door open for her, the *senhora* with the younger couple, the one with the nice clothes. I am touched by the gesture of the maids coming to the door and I stop crying to talk to them. I tell them in Spanish that she was my mother and they seem almost on the point of crying themselves.

In an article about the Portuguese character, Marcus Cheke writes that the Portuguese are a very sentimental people and likely to respond to situations on a very personal level. He tells about an incident that happened during the war, when he was attached to the British Embassy in Lisbon. A British plane flying over Portugal crashed in the mountains and all the crew were killed. When the funeral service was being performed village women strewed flowers in the grave and said, 'We are thinking of the mothers.' Cheke finds something very Portuguese in this story: this is the sort of gesture that occurs spontaneously to Portuguese people, he suggests. The maids at the Hotel Valverde seem to bear him out.

We look in the *Diário de Notícias* for a light film in English and find one by Woody Allen. We go to the cinema by Metro, and the whole project takes up enough attention for my mind to be slightly distracted from what has happened. We sit in the balcony, and watching the film is like taking aspirin to relieve pain. It is wonderful to be without it for a couple of hours. There is an intermission, and the moment the curtains come in front of the screen the aspirin wears off and the awfulness returns. Incredibly, as we go up the aisle for a drink during the intermission we meet Dr Fernandes and his wife! Of all the places in Lisbon where they might spend the evening and of all the places where we might have gone, we have both come to this cinema, and even the balcony of it! This gives my mind something else to chew on, and I am grateful for anything that comes along.

I am tired, though. The day began such a long time ago, and we have done so much, lived so long. The day began last night, or yesterday, rather. The cardiologist and the hospital were so long ago, but yet I keep reliving it. We took a taxi to the medical school. At the Embassy they wrote the address on a slip of paper. We showed it to the taxi driver in the black car with the green top, and he knew just where to go. At the medical school my typing went all to pieces because of the unfamiliar keyboard with the *a* and *z* transposed. I don't remember the rest of the room, just trying to see the typewriter through the tears. I must get some more kleenex. A box of kleenex, the new improved giant economy four-ply grief size …

I went to sleep and missed the end of the film. Afterwards young Dr Fernandes and his wife offered to drive us back to the Hotel Valverde. That was very nice of them, and we thanked them as we got out in the Rua Rodrigues Sampaio. They were sympathetic, like the hotel maids.

The next day there are other things to do, including another trip to the medical school. 'Your mamá,' says Dr Fernandes brightly, 'is *here* now.' He points with both forefingers to the floor in front of him, like someone playing 'Chopsticks' on the piano. António Fernandes must expect this information to cheer me up, but instead I burst into tears. It isn't just that my mother's corpse is lying somewhere in the Anatomy Department that makes me cry; any mention of her is enough to set me off, especially if I have not cried for 20 or

30 minutes. I mop at my eyes with a tissue while Dr Fernandes watches sympathetically.

I tell Dr Fernandes that she died of a heart attack. 'She had both legs broken when she was in her 30s,' I tell him. I feel an absurd wish to be helpful. I can never explain to him in a short time and across the language barrier who she really was, and, scarcely realising what I am doing, I tell the medical details that I think will interest him. 'As a child she had a serious streptococcus infection,' I say. Names of diseases are a kind of Esperanto; his Portuguese ear will make sense of my English Latin without translation.

Dr Fernandes insists on showing us his anatomy laboratory. It is a model of cleanliness and stainless steel. I don't want to think too closely about cadavers and medical students. He loves his job. Somebody has to do this. It's a good thing, in the long run. (My father wanted to be a doctor like his father, but this is as far as he got. He couldn't dissect cadavers. It would take a certain frame of mind, certainly.) Fernandes probably doesn't understand squeamishness, but he at least made sure that the lab was empty before we came in. This is his job and he loves it, cutting up cadavers and showing other people how to do it and how everything fits together. Fernandes is probably a good teacher. He has the necessary enthusiasm. His students will remember him later when they are surgeons. I try to seem interested. There is stainless steel everywhere.

I like António Fernandes because he is a link with my mother, in a certain strange way. He at least is going to get to see her again. It is ironic that she will still be involved in teaching, even after her death. Did she think of that? Or did she just think that education was more constructive than a funeral? Notice, students, the superior vena cava; see how it is attached to the various things it's attached to.

In all this running around and attending to things, I keep wanting to tell my mother about it, and then I remember I can't. I want to tell her about young Dr Fernandes and his stainless steel, the receptionist at the Embassy, the place we went for dinner because we couldn't bear the hotel restaurant any more. In lucid moments between bouts of crying, I think of her habit of calling things 'an interesting experience'. This is *not* an interesting experience. *Bereavement* with its three soft syllables is something relatively under control. What sits in the pit of your stomach and behind your eyes is *grief*, one sharp syllable like a rabbit chop. *Bereavement* is a word made up by someone whose mother is still alive.

We go to the Embassy again. The receptionist/secretary is extremely helpful and sympathetic. She has a Portuguese name but speaks English with what sounds like a New York accent. We take some items of clothing and give them to her to give to a charity.

We finally run out of errands and formalities and have to go home. On the night before we leave we go to another light film, this time one with Peter Sellers in it. It, too, is like aspirin to relieve pain, and although I enjoy it, I miss the ending again because I can't keep my eyes open.

We pay the hotel bill. There is a mysterious extra bill, and when I query it, they tell me it is from the fire department. The ambulances in the city are all operated by the fire department. I don't like to leave Lisbon, because I am leaving my mother behind. I know this is irrational all the time I'm thinking it. We were together here, and there seems to be something of her about the streets and buildings, the mosaic paving and the palm trees. Before we leave I go to the Avenida da Liberdade and with a great sense of purpose and concentration take some pictures of the designs in the paving. I stand on a park bench and sight carefully down at the most intricate part of the figure. Then it can't be put off any longer and we take a black and green taxi to the airport.

Lisbon hasn't changed at all, at least the central parts that a tourist sees. The same fine avenues, the same shabby-looking buildings mixed in with the glass and steel office buildings;

the same blue sky and palm trees. Do the residents of Lisbon know how delightful their city is to a northerner used to cold temperatures and bare trees? Do they take all this for granted? In another way, of course, Lisbon is quite different. I am here alone staying in a hotel on the other side of the city. I've been looking forward to coming here: it's like the fulfilment of an ambition, almost. I want to see Lisbon, memorise it, get to know it. This time I am going to hear fado and go to Belém and the Gulbenkian Museum and walk through the Alfama, the oldest section of Lisbon. This will be very different from my last visit, but closely linked, too.

I must go to see my friends at the American Embassy, but it is not in the same place as seven years ago. It has moved to a new site out on the Avenida das Forças Armadas instead of its small suite of rooms around the corner from the Hotel Valverde. The secretary, Betty, still works there, but the diplomatic staff changes every few years. Betty is actually a British subject, born in the Azores, and married to a Portuguese man. I still don't know where she got the New York accent.

I take the Metro to Entre Campos and walk in the direction of the American Embassy. This is a mistake, because the Embassy is about two miles away and the road is a fast clearway with no sidewalk. I trudge along carrying a small nylon knapsack containing boxes of chocolate for the staff. I feel silly in this no man's land in my knitted suit and my bulging knapsack and my unsuitable shoes. Finally I reach a complex of low brick buildings with low-pitched tile roofs. It looks like the country place of a well-off Roman senator. Getting into it is like getting into Fort Knox, but finally I am shown into the consular section, which is technically closed to the public at this hour of the afternoon. It's nice to see Betty again, and I meet the new vice-consul, a big man with a blond moustache. They introduce me to the Portuguese lawyer who works full-time for the Embassy. I bring out my duty-free chocolates and hand them around and we all sit and chat.

It's wonderful to see them. They are like old and dear friends and I wish we could talk for longer, but I know they're busy and I don't want to take up too much of their time. I finally leave them with their massive tin boxes of chocolate and go out onto Forças Armadas to find the right Metro station.

VII

On the way to a restaurant that advertises fado performances, I ask the taxi driver if he likes fado. 'Yes, of course,' he says proudly, 'it's our national music!'

I can't quite imagine most Lisboans going to a place like the Rio Vinho, however. It claims to be both chic and bohemian, but I don't see how it can be both. When I get there I find that it is neither. The door is barely visible under the stickers for all the credit cards accepted by the establishment. The interior is Iberian Rustic: whitewashed arches and dark wooden panelling. Although it's eight in the evening, I am the first customer. Long tables are set with white tablecloths and napkins folded like accordions in the wine glasses. At intervals down the length of three long tables there are little pairs of Portuguese and American flags. As I don't have a reservation, I am put at a small table by a pillar in the middle of the room.

I dawdle over my olives and appetisers, and before long the Americans turn up and occupy their tables. In early middle age, the men are clean-cut and wear blazers, as though they've just left their yachts in the harbour. The women have very carefully arranged hair, and something in their manner suggests a sorority reunion. On the whole, they look like the Rotary Club having an evening out, and I wonder what they are doing in Lisbon. Are they Rotarians with their wives or Pi Phis with their husbands? The question persists, and I feel well disposed toward them because I rarely see many of my countrymen now. I think fondly of my friends at the

American Embassy. Later, curiosity gets the better of me, and as one of the men walks past my table I ask him where they are from. He puts his hands familiarly on my shoulders and says, 'We're all Communists!' He is doing his navy-blazer best to be outrageous, poor man. Much later, passing my table again and perhaps fearing that I had believed him, he comes clean and tells me they are from California, but I have rather lost interest by now. They seem to be the backers of some American congressman with a Portuguese name, but I find I am brimming over with indifference.

Still later another large group comes in. They are dressed very elegantly and seem all to be Portuguese. The women wear their fur status symbols on this mild evening. The men are sleekly middle-aged with distinguished grey temples and expensive suits. By ten most of us have finished eating, but a few people are still ordering their main course. The waiters practise a kind of choreography as they bring food from the kitchen, put it on a serving table, and with many flourishes arrange the food on plates. But the singing is supposed to begin at ten, and soon after the hour I feel a gust of cold air from the overhead ventilation, and the lights dim.

On this signal five men walk out from the kitchen holding guitars and sit on chairs on the other side of my table, facing away from me. From somewhere a woman appears; this according to my programme, is Maria Isabel, and the waiter whispers that she is the daughter of the oldest guitarist. She begins by facing the semi-circle of guitarists and arranging her black shawl around her shoulders. The black shawl is an important garment for all fado singers, I have read. A famous *fadista* of the last century – the Jenny Lind of fado – wore a black shawl, and now a black shawl with long fringe is nearly as essential as the guitar. The men begin playing their guitars, three of the rounded Portuguese type and two of the more familiar Spanish type. Maria Isabel turns and sings to her audience, and as the performance is in the round, she pivots slowly as she sings, addressing first one part of the house and then another.

It is very pleasant to listen to, even if it has been a long time coming. I have had a meal, but there are still some black olives left, and so I keep nibbling them. Maria Isabel sings to the ladies in their fur coats and the Communist Rotarian Pi Phis, and everyone seems to enjoy the music. Some of the Portuguese audience know the songs and join in the chorus. She sings several numbers, which all seem to be of a lamenting nature and deeply felt. Now and then there is a Moorish wail which reminds me that it couldn't be Edith Piaf or an American blues singer after all. I could listen to it all night, but after about fifteen minutes the lights come up again and the guitarists and singer all file back into the kitchen.

The waiters now fly into action, carrying food briskly in from the kitchen (past the guitarists, visible through the small windows in the swinging doors) and taking empty dishes and plates from the tables. If one of them were a fraction off course they would all collide in a heap of broken crockery, but they have practised and have it down to a split-second art.

Soon the lights dim and the guitarists come out again, this time with a different singer, Teresa, who looks older than Maria Isabel and also wears a black shawl and seems similarly careworn. The pattern is repeated as the night goes on: intervals when the waiters make up for lost time and performances by new singers, each more mature and worn down by life than the last. The little semi-circle of guitars is like a chorus egging her on. 'Tell it like it is,' the guitars seem to say. 'Life is hard, love is fleeting, sorrow is here to stay. Tell how it is. Oh, tell it!'

During one interval the American group all get up and leave to go and enliven another chic and bohemian fado restaurant.

If one traditional fado subject is one's mother, I could write them a few fados! They could have as much melancholy and *saudade* as any home-grown fado. 'My Mother's Shawl' and 'A Fado For My Mother' seem to be old standards. There is one called 'Black Mother' and another is simply 'My Mother', *Minha Mãe*. I could write them some absolutely crackerjack fados! They could be about Lisbon, too, and nostalgia and things going wrong. I could turn out a dozen; I could start a sub-genre. I couldn't perform them, and somebody else would have to provide the guitar accompaniment, and the words wouldn't be in Portuguese, but I could make up for those drawbacks with *saudade* by the bushel.

At the medical school they told me that they used bodies for about a year and then committed them for burial. I replied that I preferred to have the body cremated so that I could take the ashes back to my mother's home. Although cremation is not the common custom in Portugal, there is a crematorium in Lisbon. Ten months after she died the medical school wrote that they would let me know as soon as possible when they would be finished with the cadaver.

After that I enquired every few months about the plans for final disposal of the body, but I never had an answer. I occasionally wrote friendly letters to young Dr Fernandes, enquiring about his family and mentioning my concern at hearing nothing from his department. Three years after my last letter from the medical school, I wrote to the American Embassy in Lisbon to ask for the name of a local lawyer who might deal with the medical school on my behalf. By this time vice-consuls had come and gone and the Embassy had moved to a different site, out near Sete Rios. The new vice-consul contacted the Anatomy Department and found that the body would be available for cremation in six months, in July, when the Anatomy Department would contact me.

In November of that year I wrote to the Embassy saying that I had not yet heard from the Anatomy Department. In March of the following year I sent a registered letter to the head of the Anatomy Department (with a copy to the vice-consul at the American Embassy), but it was returned unopened. In April I wrote again to the vice-consul, asking if she could find an explanation for the lack of communication from the Anatomy Department. My mother had been dead for five years, and I wanted to finish the business. I was beginning to be alarmed. Had they forgotten? Had they lost the body or disposed of it in some other way? Why didn't they contact me? Even young Dr Fernandes, who was no longer so young, didn't answer my letters. Was the Portuguese post office to blame? Sometimes I had disturbing dreams. In one, I protested to the medical school that I wanted my mother's body back, and someone roughly handed me a large, bulky plastic sack. 'Here!' he snapped, 'take it!'

I learned from the Embassy that as the death had occurred more than a year ago, the Portuguese Bureau of Vital Statistics was required to obtain a court order to register the death. 'We regret to have to advise you of these further delays. We will continue to follow on this matter with the authorities involved, and will keep you advised so that we can coordinate the date of the ceremony with you,' wrote the vice-consul. At least someone in Lisbon was receiving my letters and agreed that the Anatomy Department should be goaded into action. In July I heard from the Embassy that they had had no word from the Portuguese authorities. Finally, in March of the following year, I heard from the vice-consul, a new one, the fourth, who wrote me that I would have to present evidence to the Portuguese authorities that I was my mother's next-of-kin. Anyone might think that as I had donated the body in the first place it would be reasonable to return the remains to me, but this was not enough for the Ministry of Justice, in whose hands the case now was.

I spent several days that spring writing affidavits and taking them to the Portuguese and American Embassies in London to be adorned with ribbons and seals. I was indeed my mother's daughter; I supplied the names and place of residence of her parents; I sent photocopies of her original bequeathal form leaving her body to the Indiana Anatomical Board and the codicil in her handwriting on the back. Now and again I would receive packets of documents from the Ministry of Justice in Lisbon, mostly photocopies of things I had sent them. They sent me extracts of Indiana laws concerning inheritance; they needed a copy of her birth certificate; they wanted my brother's address. As the summer wore on, typewritten letters beginning 'Dear Lady' would arrive from the Ministry of Justice, and there were other handwritten letters, whose sloppiness, together with the fact that they were in Portuguese, defeated me and I had to send photocopies to the Embassy in Lisbon for an explanation.

Sometimes I imagined the Portuguese officials poring over the papers. I wondered what real use it was for them to know that William Everett Reed and Grace Myrtle Reed, née Chambers, both born in Indiana, had had a child, Fern Lorraine, on December 9, 1902, in Washington Township, Hendricks County, in the State of Indiana. The record was filed on December 31, 1902, and I pictured my young, dark-haired grandfather unable to get to the Danville courthouse before that because of the muddy or snow-blocked dirt roads. I sent a photocopy of Fern's birth certificate to Portugal and they sent me back a photocopy of my photocopy and a Portuguese translation of it.

At the Portuguese Consulate in London, I was taken from the waiting-room and down a long corridor to an office where a pleasant-looking woman was sitting behind a typewriter. After all the letters to and from anonymous officials at the Ministry of Justice, here was a human being. Perhaps she would take a personal interest in my story. She already had some of the papers relating to the case and was prepared to type in Portuguese what I dictated to her in English. 'My mother died in Lisbon six years ago,' I told her before we began, 'and her body was donated to a medical school. I just want her body back so that it can be cremated. In the beginning they said it would be about a year.' I was trying to make a personal appeal, as mentioned by so many writers on Portugal, who say that the Portuguese people above all others are susceptible to this approach. 'I want to take her ashes back to Indiana and have them buried by her parents' graves,' I added. 'That was what she requested, and I'd like to carry out that request.' What could be simpler? Practically anything else, apparently. But the woman at the typewriter seemed very sympathetic.

'We're so busy here,' she sighed. 'We're short-staffed and several people have been off sick. We have such a backlog.'

So she wanted sympathy from *me*. I tried to look interested. 'We're months behind,' she went on. 'We've had these papers' – she indicated my bulging dossier – 'since last winter.'

I winced. Somebody would be dealing with *my* ashes before I had finished with these.

I dictated the necessary affidavit. I had brought a briefcase full of all the documents I could think of, in case they wanted to photocopy anything else. The woman read back to me in English what she had written in Portuguese. I looked carefully at the Portuguese text and then signed my name at the end of it.

By September I was communicating with the Embassy in Lisbon by telephone. Betty would phone with some piece of news or a request for information, and sometimes I would hear from the new vice-consul who had just arrived at the Embassy. A Portuguese lawyer who worked full-time for the Embassy was working hard on the case. The anniversary of my mother's death came around again; it was January now, seven years after that terrible night when she vanished before the ambulance and the cardiologist arrived at the Hotel Valverde.

Two weeks later John, the vice-consul, telephoned from Lisbon to say that I could name a date for the cremation. It seemed hardly believable. The cremation? No more documents going back and forth across the Bay of Biscay in registered letters? The actual cremation in the Cemitério do Alto do São João, where there is a crematorium, though little used? I looked at my diary and named a date at random, a Monday three weeks away. Can this be The Date finally? Am I really naming it?

I make some phone calls about flights to Lisbon, I have a hotel reservation made, I get some escudos at the bank. (The Hotel Valverde is an excellent hotel, but nothing would induce me to stay there again.) I'm really going! I get out my suitcase and decide what to take. I write to people and tell them I'll be away from home for a while. I'm really finally going! I have to find out how to get to Gatwick Airport by train from my part of London. I decide to get some presents for my three friends at the American Embassy, and then I decide to get them in the duty-free shop at Gatwick. (John, when asked point-blank, admitted to preferring chocolate to other duty-free possibilities. Chocolate it shall be!) My tickets come in the mail, British Airways, leaving from Gatwick and coming back to Heathrow, too bad if you want to leave your car at the airport.

And then I'm at the airport finding the right desk, circulating with my supermarket trolley as though I have just bought my suitcase. (In fact it was my mother's suitcase, one of a set of three with her initials on them. The lock combination was suggested by the saleslady at Ayres, who said that most people set the combination for their birthdays. It's still 12-9, December the ninth, for I have never bothered to change it.)

I'm free of the suitcase now; it's making its own way to the airplane, bound for Lisbon for the second time. I go through gates and barriers, I show my passport here and my boarding pass there. I choose three large tin boxes of chocolate at the duty-free shop. Big as they are, they fail to express my gratitude to the dogged staff at the Embassy, but they will have to do for the moment.

The curious thing, I reflect, is that the 'personal touch' mentioned by Marcus Cheke and other writers on Portugal didn't work with the Portuguese people involved, except for Jaime, the lawyer at the American Embassy, and of course those hotel maids. It had no noticeable effect on the Portuguese Consulate in London or the Ministry of Justice in Lisbon. It had absolutely no effect at all on the medical school of the New University of Lisbon or even on young (now substantially older) Dr Fernandes. The spectacle of a daughter petitioning for the return of her mother's corpse might be expected to move anyone even slightly given to sentimentality. Marcus Cheke in 'The Portuguese Character' speaks of 'the all-pervading sentimentality of their outlook on life' and adds, 'in truth, the mainspring of their thoughts and actions is the heart.' The people who did respond to this situation were the reputedly hard-headed and practical Americans. So much for national stereotypes.

Mother would have liked this restaurant with the candlelight and leather chairs and good linen. This is the kind of restaurant where you don't pour your own wine. It sits in an ice bucket and when your glass begins to look empty a passing waiter executing one of his precision routines lifts the bottle with a flourish and pours a little into your glass. When there is still half an inch left in the bottom of the bottle, the waiter whisks it away to the kitchen so that you will not be offended by the dregs. Waiters in black jackets prepare the plates and other waiters in burgundy jackets serve the plates to the diners. My table is near the centre of activity. I watch a black-jacketed waiter expertly fillet a fish. The vertebrae and other inedible parts are piled quickly onto another plate and disappear into the kitchen with the next passing waiter. Mother would have enjoyed watching their skill and teamwork. (Once in a similar Spanish restaurant she delightedly noticed that the well-drilled waiters were all walking in a quick 2/4 time.)

What strikes me now about fado is that, although the subject matter may be very melancholy, the effect is not depressing. They are tuneful songs about Life, but if they were really depressing no one would want to listen to them.

The blues must be like this: you don't listen to Bessie Smith in order to be depressed. Countess Almaviva in *The Marriage of Figaro* sings what I now realise is a fado, '*Porg'ia amor*' and later another song full of *saudade*, '*Dov'è sono*', but they are far from depressing for the audience. All these songs are about feeling and about getting through rough patches and having bad luck and disappointments. Perhaps they are popular because they give the audience courage for their own rough patches and bad luck. Or alternatively, the audience can feel relieved that this is somebody else's rough patch. 'I don't know why you went away,' the last singer wails in an oddly catchy song. The Portuguese contingent tonight sing along with the choruses and can understand the rest of the words, and they are clearly enjoying themselves.

One is simply about the typical Portuguese house – 'Uma Casa Portuguesa' – and some of the fados are even about singing fados. 'I Want to Sing You a Fado' is the title of one of them, and another goes, 'I will sing until my voice aches' – not her throat, her *voice*. Some songs try to define fado: 'It is love and jealousy, ashes and fire too, sorrow and sin. The fado – it's all that excites, all that is sad'. The songs are about maturity, too, and make a change from adolescent Anglo-American pop music.

'My Old Kentucky Home' must be a fado. And how about 'Lipstick on Your Collar'? Fados are everywhere. Is '*Die Lorelei*' a fado? It's about being inexplicably sad, about being afflicted with *saudade*. I decide that it's probably a fado.

The next day the streets seem full of fado singers. Every woman I pass, except for the very young ones, seems to be a potential *fadista*. Some of them even wear shawls like the singers' last night. They look as though their lives would yield up a few fados. I imagine them spending their evenings at restaurants like the Rio Vinho, more or less chic, more or less bohemian.

VIII

Tomorrow is going to be a hard day, but for the moment I do not feel it. I only surmise that I am in for something, like someone who feels fine but has to undergo an operation and knows that there may be some pain in the near future, if not just now. Today is another bright, bracing day, like a perfect English summer day, or like a sunny day in the spring in Indiana before the Turkish-bath heat of the summer.

I am going out to Belém to see what's there. I already know roughly what's there: the Tower of Belém, the Monument to the Discoveries, and the 16th-century Monastery of the Jerónimos, and I want to see them all. I take the train from the Cais do Sodré out along the coast to Belém station and walk the rest of the way.

The Tower of Belém is a vest-pocket castle done in cake icing. In the great days when Portuguese explorers set sail to discover the next stretch of the African coast or the far Indies, the Tower of Belém was well out into the Tagus, but now it is approached from a park and then a wooden bridge. The guidebook says that it was built between 1515 and 1521 and is a classic example of the Manueline style. King Manuel the Fortunate gave his name to a peculiar style of architecture and decoration that is uniquely Portuguese. In the old days it must have looked like a stone ship cross-wise against the current. The castle rises from what looks very much like a ship's deck with guardhouses spaced around it. The squat, square castle keep is crenellated on several levels and there are some projecting covered balconies supported by machicolations.

There are corbelled turrets at the corners of the Tower and the 'deck' below it. Below decks is a large chamber with gun-ports around the walls just above the waterline. The effect is that of a late-medieval aircraft carrier.

Some of the crenellations turn out to be shields with the cross of Portugal on them. They are dished in a way that emphasises their decorativeness, although they are clearly part of the defensive fortifications. Nautical motifs are everywhere: ropes and knots, fish and shells. The roofs of the turrets are all ribbed like shells, and at the level of the 'deck' there are lines of masonry 'rope' encircling the whole structure – a string course, so to speak. It is as though the castle and the deck have been lashed together to withstand any storms that may blow into the estuary. Elsewhere the arches, capitals, balustrades and finials of the building are decorated until their function is to be vehicles for decoration.

I wander through the Tower, losing count of the floors so that when I come to what I think is the top there is still a further storey. I wonder if they lit a beacon at the top to warn Lisbon of attack from the sea. I wonder how many men stayed here at one time and what use it was actually put to.

On the way out of the Tower I find four American tourists, one taking a picture of the other three. I recognise a dilemma of tourists everywhere and offer to take a picture of all four of them. They are two middle-aged married couples, nice people with a pleasant manner. I don't ask them where they're from, although I know that if I asked they would gladly tell me and express a polite interest in whatever I cared to tell them about myself. They are probably Midwesterners. We are an artless folk who do not bother to make up silly lies to tell strangers in foreign restaurants. I am told by the camera owner which button to press, and then I sight at them through the view-finder. They pose in front of the doors and I try to get a bit of the Tower in. Thank you, they say, and I reply that I know how it is, 'You always end up with pictures with one person missing,' and they laugh amicably.

It is a tiny encounter, an insignificant encounter, but at the same time I take pleasure in it. It is the pleasure of being able to communicate with friendly strangers with whom one shares something, however basic. I am not feeling very cheerful today, but it cheers me up to help these four tourists enjoy their vacation. ('Look, this one's of all four of us. This woman came up to us at the Tower of Belém and offered to take our picture.')

Just as Lisbon is full of places where you can look out over the city and see other places from which other people are looking out over the city, there are several things to climb in Belém. Not far from the Tower, across the park and beyond a yacht harbour, is the Monument to the Discoveries and to Prince Henry the Navigator. Part of it is shaped like the prow of a ship with Prince Henry standing at the front like a figurehead with a model ship in his hands. Behind him stretch out the sorts of people who followed him: soldiers, scientists, missionaries and artists. The rest of the monument is a stark structure 10 or 12 storeys high. You go in through large glass doors which seem small, like doors between the paws of the Sphinx. You buy a ticket that is eye-catching enough to frame and take the elevator as far as it goes and then climb several more flights of stairs until you come out onto the roof of the Monument, where you can look over a parapet at the Tagus, the statue of Christ the King on the opposite bank, the April 24 Bridge, the Tower of Belém, Lisbon in the distance, the yachts below, a restaurant in its expensive little lagoon, and the Jerónimos Monastery.

There is something compelling about high places where one's perspective changes and things that were large become tiny and indistinguishable from other tiny things; enormous buildings become little interruptions on the horizon. Finally I satisfy my curiosity in all the directions of the compass and get back down to ground level. Outside on the mosaic paving in front of the Monument, I see the surroundings freshly for the second time today. The tiny things are large again and the lagoon with the restaurant in the middle has ceased to be a shallow blue handkerchief. Life is down on the ground again.

The third thing on my list in Belém is the Monastery. I buy another entrance ticket that is suitable for framing and wander around the cloister. This huge monastery was built by King Manuel the Fortunate as a thanks offering for Vasco da Gama's discovery of a sea route to India. Even before it was built, there was an altar to Our Lady of the Navigators here where Vasco da Gama is said to have spent the night praying before he left for the long voyage which resulted in the first Western contact with India. It was the night of July 7, 1497, and the journey that began the next day lasted for ten and a half months, during which a third of the crew of 170 died of scurvy and one of his four ships was destroyed. When Camoens wrote his epic about the voyage it was still within living memory.

So Vasco da Gama came here when he was apprehensive about the next day. I have a fellow-feeling with Vasco da Gama. This is as good a place as any to come when you have provisioned your ships and hired your sailors and you're just waiting for daylight and the tide. It's a good place to come to climb up on top of things and exercise your faculty for getting things in perspective, even if it is only large bridges and statues for the time being. I study Belém as though I am taking a course in it: Intro to Portuguese History, perhaps, with special reference to modern personal applications thereof.

The voyages of exploration in the 15th and 16th centuries were at least as daring as the space explorations of our own time. The Tower of Belém was a kind of launching pad. The Portuguese explorers sailed off the map and found treacherous strangers and merciless weather. They came back and re-drew the map. 'The Cape of Good Hope' is the public relations name for what the sailors themselves called 'The Cape of Storms'. King João (who had not been in the storms) changed the name, as he had also changed the name of Belém from Restelo.

The Portuguese explorers not only discovered large areas of the globe, but were the first Europeans to see the stars of the Southern Hemisphere. They explored in all directions and dimensions. Even Christopher Columbus learned everything he knew about navigation from the Portuguese. He married a Portuguese woman and used her father's charts. He might have sailed under the patronage of the Portuguese king except that he was regarded as an amateur and an upstart in that land of advanced navigators. He was just lucky in the 15th-century pastime of playing blind man's buff with whole continents.

They explored the Northern Hemisphere, too. Labrador was named after a man from the Azores, and in 1501 an explorer described the Eskimos. The Portuguese visited Greenland, Nova Scotia and Newfoundland and gave names to Conception Bay and Cape Bonavista. Compared to the Portuguese, Odysseus looks absurdly inept. How could anyone get lost in the Mediterranean for ten years? In ten years the Portuguese could have sailed around the world several times, discovering most of it as they went. In his preface to Canto I of *The Lusiads*, Camoens wrote: 'Let us hear no more then of Ulysses and Aeneas and their long journeyings, no more of Alexander and Trajan and their famous victories. My theme is the daring and renown of the Portuguese, to whom Neptune and Mars alike give homage.' Camoens himself led an active life. He lost one eye at Ceuta and travelled to the Far East as far as the Moluccas and Macau, where he was appointed to the post of Trustee for the Dead and Absent. (What did Luís Camoens do as Trustee for the Dead and Absent? Did he recover bodies from the Moluccans and the Macauians? 'I understand our brothers José and João have fallen on your territory. Could we have their mortal remains back, please?')

In 1512 Timor was discovered, and the name was never revised like that of the Cape of Good Hope. Fear it was named and Fear it remained. Once the explorers got to their farthest point, how did they look upon their voyage back? Did some of them settle in distant places because they couldn't face the return trip? When they got out on their watery limb, they put their trust in their astrolabes and sextants and Our Lady of the Navigators and came back, according to Camoens, to Belém in the mouth of the 'friendly Tagus' to report to the King and bring him cloves and silks and silver; nutmeg from the Banda Islands and sandalwood from Timor.

The huge two-storey cloister at the Jerónimos encloses a charming garden in the garth, and in the centre is a tinkling fountain. This fountain must be new, because the postcards and illustrations in souvenir books show a simple round flowerbed in the middle. The arches and columns of this cloister are so richly decorated that it makes the little marzipan Tower of Belém look positively spartan. No doubt the monks used to walk here lost in thought, but even without thinking of anything in particular it is easy to get lost. You would suppose that the four-square design, open in the middle so that you can see around corners and see where you have been and where you are going, could not be simpler, but yet I have lost track of the number of times I have wandered the circuit, and I keep passing doorways I have not noticed before. I am more preoccupied than I had realised.

The pious gloom of the church is filled with baroquely Gothic shapes and ornate columns that the guidebook compares to stalagmites. The tombs of both Vasco da Gama and Camoens are here, 'The latter empty since 1755,' says the guidebook, 'the year when the terrible earthquake caused the ashes of the poetic genius of *Os Lusiádas* to be scattered to the four winds.' I try to think how this happened, a crack forming in the massive sarcophagus and the ashes trickling out and blowing away. Ashes? Perhaps the writer only means 'remains', in whatever state. But another writer, William C. Atkinson, who translated *The Lusiads*, says that in 1880 'his presumed remains were removed to the church at Belém that Manuel the Fortunate had built to celebrate the discovery of the sea route to India, on the same spot whence da Gama sailed and to which he returned. There they keep company with those of da Gama himself, his distant kinsman and hero.' Still another writer reports that Camoens died in such poverty that he had to be buried in a pauper's grave in a borrowed shroud. (A *borrowed* shroud?) So the remains of Camoens or someone else or nothing at all may be inside the sarcophagus; you can take your choice. A Trustee for the Dead and Absent is needed here.

Elsewhere I find a little bust and plinth in honour of the poet Fernando Pessoa (1888-1935), bilingual in Portuguese and English, writing mainly in Portuguese under his own name and at least four pseudonyms. A quotation in Portuguese from his work is chiselled on the monument. It reads:

> To see the fields and the river
> It is not enough just to open the window.
> Not being blind is not sufficient
> To see the trees and flowers.

With my imperfect knowledge of Portuguese it seems fresh and profound until I translate it into English, where it has to take its chances with all the other sentiments and philosophies I have heard in my own language.

It is odd what a fine line there can be between the profound and the commonplace. Often what tips the balance one way or the other is only the way of expressing the idea. If the language is original the thought seems original; clumsy language, and the thought seems pedestrian, yet it may be the same thought. I stare at the incised quotation, trying to decide why the idea sounds appealing in Portuguese, even though it is noticeably banal.

Later, after I leave Belém, I discover that I have missed the National Museum of Archaeology and Ethnology, which is also housed in the Jerónimos Monastery. It contains Roman mosaic floors and I am sorry that I didn't know it was there. However, I will probably not bother to go back to it because there are too many areas in and around Lisbon where I haven't been even once. I will save it for another visit, whenever that may be. Furthermore, I have missed the Naval Museum… It seems premature to be compiling a list of things to visit 'next time', but the tourist is always making lists of priorities; this today, that next week, and that some day when it's raining and everything else is closed.

There are more little Carnival children in Belém, many having their pictures taken by proud parents in the Praça do Impéro out in front of the Monastery. There are more Zorros and more fairy queens, and late in the afternoon I see one little boy of 5 or 6 dressed as a Renaissance gentleman in doublet and hose who is so tired that his father is carrying him. He wears a fine satiny cape, like the Zorros. Perhaps he is meant to be a 16th-century king, or even Camoens. He looks wonderfully incongruous in his striped doublet, curled up half asleep in his father's arms.

This public tenderness of parents toward their children impresses me. As a stranger here, I too am treated with patience and sympathy. I have experienced a good deal of kindness at first-hand, and I see more of it around me. Although the traffic in Lisbon is hair-raising, on my walks around the city I have seen blind people confidently tapping their white canes along the sidewalk. When they come to a kerb they stop walking but keep tapping their canes, and in a moment some passer-by steps forward to help them across the street.

One evening as I was walking along the Rua Garrett, a man on the opposite sidewalk threw himself into the street and rolled over and over, coming to rest motionless beside a parked car. As three or four pedestrians approached him, he rolled vigorously out into the middle of the street. Before any cars could come along they carried the man to the sidewalk and someone went to phone for a doctor. Meanwhile other passers-by had collected some loose change that had fallen out of the man's pockets and returned it to him.

I remember the warm-heartedness of some Portuguese people seven years ago, like the hotel maids who came to our door and a doctor at the medical school who told me that he believed in the existence of the soul because the organs in a dead body were quite different from those in a living body; there was something very odd, he said, about the transformation that occurs at death. It was more than just the cessation of life. I found his remarks very soothing. By saying anything at all about death he was helping me to think about it and grasp what had happened late at night in the Hotel Valverde. It was both death and the sudden disappearance of my mother that had shocked me. I had seen the Reaper at work and felt the breeze as he passed.

Tomorrow lurks in the back of my mind. It is something to be faced and planned for. It will be a melancholy experience, but at least not as wrenching as a normal funeral would be. How many funerals happen seven years after the death? I've already been through all the funeral feelings in great detail. I have to be at the Embassy fairly early; I have to wait for their phone call. I set my alarm clock earlier and check the hotel breakfast times. I lay out some clothes to wear, taking a few items out of my mother's suitcase, fixing the numbers on her birthday to unlock it.

I have brought along a little New Testament and Psalms that belonged to my mother. It is one of the two or three dozen Bibles she collected and used. I know she used them because in all of them there are underlinings and brackets in the margins. I have brought this little pocket Bible mainly as a talisman, but in the evening in my hotel room I turn on all the lights so that there is enough illumination to read by. In this copy most of the underlining, in red ballpoint and turquoise pencil, is in the Epistles, especially those to the Ephesians and the Philippians ('I have learned, in whatsoever state I am, therewith to be content' [Phil. 4:11]). I page through the little volume looking for my mother's underlinings. Even her underlining is distinctive! I could pick it out from others if I were shown a page with underlining by different people on it. Her flowing bracket drawn down the side of a paragraph is unlike any mark ever made by anyone else.

I wonder when she was reading this little New Testament with its silvery page edges, and what was happening in her life at the time. Was it just for her own use or was she preparing a Sunday school lesson for one of her adult classes? This multi-coloured underlining is so typical of her that it makes me smile. Perhaps because of her years as a teacher she was always fond of pencils and ballpoint pens in as many different colours as possible. She spent much of her life with a coloured pencil in one hand – grading papers or jotting down annotations on music scores – and then at some point she looked at Philippians 3:13 and underlined in turquoise 'forgetting those things which are behind, and reaching forth unto those things which are before', and now I read it in this hotel room as though it is a message from her. All the underlinings become moments of contact with her mind, and I leaf through the little book looking for her.

IX

I get out to Sete Rios the next morning and walk to the Embassy. Jaime meets me at the door and introduces me to the director of the Boa Hora funeral agency. We shake hands and Jaime translates our remarks. We seem to state this afternoon's plans to each other interspersed with polite expressions of goodwill. We know what we are doing. We will act in concert; we know what to expect of each other. Above all, we reiterate the appointed time. When the funeral director has to leave and attend to other business, we shake hands again and part until this afternoon.

I go through the Fort Knox-like procedure to get into the consular office and then follow Jaime into his office. We talk, but he has to make some phone calls about another matter, so I sit in front of his desk and look around the room at the pictures of his family and the shelves of Portuguese law books. Jaime is a trim man with a goatee. His English is good, and he has a certificate on the wall to prove it. He has been around Americans long enough to pick up some of their informal ways, at least during working hours. Between phone calls he remarks cheerfully, 'I make my living by bureaucracy, but I hate it!' Jaime finishes his phone calls and we talk some more about the strange case that is about to come to an end.

'What did the people at the medical school think they were doing?' I ask him. 'Why didn't they answer my letters?'

'Well, you know,' Jaime says with a tone of annoyance, 'those doctors are all very nice people and they're all experts in their field, but they are no good at paperwork. They found out that they hadn't filed the right papers when your mother died – when they first got the body – and nobody took responsibility for doing it later.' Jaime is a professional filer of papers and I can sense his disdain for people who are lazy about their bureaucratic duties. 'They thought that if they just ignored the problem it would go away!'

'I began to think that they'd done something else with the body. I was afraid that they'd already disposed of it without telling me.' This was a fear that seemed vaguely irrational to me, and I had not confided it to many people, but it had often occurred to me.

'Yes,' says Jaime, 'we wondered too. The previous vice-consul – Sheila – took a personal interest in the case, and one day we both went to the medical school and asked to see the body to be sure they really did still have it. They'd made so many excuses.'

'Excuses? What kind of excuses?'

'Oh, all kinds of excuses,' Jaime says with distaste. 'They said that they liked to keep some bodies longer than others because some bodies are preserved better than others, things like that. So your, eh, mother's body lasted longer than some others. That's what they told us.'

'But they told me they used them for about a year! This has been seven years now! They *knew* I was waiting to hear from them! When would they have ever done anything if you hadn't pressured them?'

'Well,' says Jaime shrugging, 'never. I'm sorry you have to have this bad impression of the Portuguese.'

'No, that's all right, it's not all the Portuguese. I rather like them, in fact. But you *went* there?'

'Yes. We said enough is enough. Sheila and I went there and told them we wanted to see the body.'

I look at his law books and wonder if this counts as habeas corpus. 'I wonder if you met Dr Fernandes. He was …'

'Dr Fernandes! Oh yes, we met him. He certainly loves his

job. He gave us a guided tour of his department.' Jaime looks uncomfortable at the memory. 'In law school I had to take a course in … in …'

'Forensic pathology?' I suggest.

'Yes, forensic pathology. I nearly failed the course because I found every excuse I could to avoid going to the class. We had lectures by doctors and surgeons, and we, eh, had to look at bodies and different injuries …'

I sympathise with Jaime and his squeamishness, Jaime a quiet and gentle family man who files papers in the right places for a living. 'I wouldn't like it either,' I tell him.

'Well, so we went there, and Dr Fernandes showed us around, and then he pulled open a big drawer in the wall …'

'I never heard about this,'I say.

'We didn't want to tell you everything,' Jaime says. 'It was rather disturbing for us, actually. When we came outside again, a funny thing happened. Sheila asked me for a cigarette, and I knew she didn't smoke.'

I'm very touched by what lengths Jaime and the previous vice-consul went to on my behalf. They didn't have to do all this; it's not in the Constitution. They must have been very determined, going to the medical school and demanding to see their cadaver and not taking no for an answer. The excuses had not worked; they refused to be fobbed off. I feel a great affection for them both. They must have cancelled their other engagements one afternoon and set out in an Embassy car for the Campo dos Mártires da Pátria. I see in my mind's eye the set of their jaws. And they did it because they had taken a personal interest in this macabre case and wanted to see justice done. There is really no way I can thank them adequately. The boxes of chocolate are a mere token of a token. And where is Sheila now? Off somewhere on another musical chair of the diplomatic service.

'If you hadn't done that for me, I could never have done it myself. I'm extremely grateful to you and the others here.'

'I hope it will give you a better impression of Portugal.'

Poor Jaime is embarrassed on behalf of his countrymen on the basis of the glaring inefficiency of a few of them, perhaps only one of them if the maze of responsibility could be untangled.

'But I like Portugal, really,' I assure him again. 'I like Lisbon, and the people I've met have been very nice.' In truth, I'm not sure why I am so attached to Lisbon, considering my experiences here. One way and another, it's a special place.

It's time for me to leave and let Jaime get on with his other business. As it is, I'm going to take up much of his afternoon; I don't need to spoil his whole morning, too.

'Come back this afternoon at one-forty-five sharp. The Embassy car will be ready then,' Jaime says.

I go to look for Betty, but on the way I meet John and we stand and talk in the middle of the big open-plan main office and then drift back to his private office. As I am about to leave, the consul from the adjoining office comes in and introduces herself. She is Mary Ann and tells me that she too has worked on the case, as have many of the Embassy staff at one time or another. 'We'll all be thinking of you this afternoon,' she tells me warmly, and once again I am deeply touched by the kindness of people I haven't met before. Mary Ann tells me that everyone is glad for me that the whole thing is finally at an end. Have I met the chief consul? I am taken to meet him, in still another office, this one larger and with more plants and places to sit than the others. We sit on a sofa and talk and I thank them again.

'We're glad to have a satisfied customer,' he jokes.

On the way out Mary Ann, who is from Indiana, introduces me to another consul who has also been involved with the case. She too tells me that she is glad that it's finally over. I should think they would all be happy to get back to routine visa matters. Finally, when I have thanked everyone again, profusely but inadequately, Mary Ann shows me to the door. Hoosiers together, we exchange place-names and other passwords from the State we are both absent from.

Now I have to kill some time before I go back to the Embassy. I have in mind a light lunch, in fact I have brought it with me. I have some nut-and-fruit snack bars, because I'm not hungry enough for a whole meal. All I need is a café of some sort where I can buy a drink and eat my bars. I go back through the Fort Knox gate and reclaim my camera, which was confiscated when I first went in with Jaime. When I get back out onto the fast road between Sete Rios and Entre Campos, I wonder where I am going to find this café. It certainly isn't around here. The roundabout at Sete Rios is the size of two or three football fields, and it seems to be the terminus for about 90 buses. To the south, however, the road curves, and I hope that out of sight around that bend there may be a modest café.

Out of sight around the bend is one of the swankiest hotels in Lisbon, with flags fluttering outside the entrance. It will be an agreeable place to while away an hour and a half. I go in and find a bar and coffee lounge which could be in any country in the world. This hotel is like the United Nations building in New York – it is neutral territory removed from the world around it and probably has its own post office in the basement, with its own stamps. The one clue that it is in Portugal is that the list of drinks is in Portuguese. I ask for an orange juice and sit at a bamboo and glass coffee table, the only customer in the large bar. Then I discreetly eat my two snack bars for lunch and have a good cup of milky coffee.

I watch the clock and carefully time my return to the Embassy. Jaime is waiting at the entrance again, and exactly on time, the chauffeur-driven Embassy car appears. On the way to the cemetery Jaime tells me that he still feels bad about his own mother's death. She died six years ago at 74 after being hit by a bus. 'What makes me feel so bad about it,' he tells me sadly, 'is that she was going to buy dog food for my dog when she was hit. I blame myself. I feel guilty about it.'

Yes, of course he would. 'You shouldn't blame yourself,' I tell him.

We arrive at the cemetery in the Alto do São João district in eastern Lisbon, and Jaime tells the driver to wait for us. This is it, the date I have set, and it is finally about to happen. Behind the high wall it is like an Italian cemetery, a city of white classical-looking mausoleums. They look like massively built gazebos for the backyard of Blenheim Palace and seem weirdly inhabited, as though there should be house numbers and door knockers on them. I meet the funeral director again and two or three assistants. We all walk the 50 yards or so to a little round building with glass walls and *CREMATORIUM* written in ornate capital letters around the top. It is further embellished with a frieze of skulls in what strikes me as morbid taste. In the bare little room a coffin sits on a metal trestle. It is a simple wooden coffin stained a reddish colour. I go forward and touch it while Jaime and the other men hang back, staying outside the doorway.

I am taken by surprise. Something happens that I didn't expect. At the sight of the coffin I begin to cry uncontrollably. It is exactly as though my mother had just died instead of seven years and one month ago. Her body is there, inside that box. She has been here in Lisbon all this time. I am closer to her now than I have been since that terrible night. But then, this is only her body and not really *her*. I rest one hand on the lid of the pine coffin and these emotions that I thought I had finished with come back, fresh as new. I have already worked through all this in the normal way during the year after my mother died. Where is this all coming from now? Is grief like malaria, so that you can keep having attacks of it if you have once been infected?

I had thought that I might read some appropriate Biblical passage during this time before the coffin goes behind the curtain, and so I get out the little white Bible. It is impossible to read it because of the tears in my eyes. When I wipe them away, more come. I step back to where Jaime is standing. By withdrawing somewhat from the coffin, I get the tears under control for the moment.

'I didn't expect this – to cry like this,' I say to him.

'It's perfectly natural,' he says.

'Yes, but I've already had all this grief seven years ago,' I say. 'It was seven years ago. You would think …'

'That doesn't matter. This is a perfectly normal reaction.'

I need to talk to Jaime. I can't just stand by the coffin and cry the whole time. I show him the little Bible, but I can't speak. I turn to the fly-leaf where Fern wrote her name.

'I understand,' he says softly. 'It was her Bible.'

I try to tell him a little about her, but my voice keeps failing me. I say that she was a teacher and a Quaker.

'Sheila was a Quaker, too,' Jaime says, 'from Philadelphia.'

My mind momentarily flickers over this detail. Then I go forward again and stand by the coffin. I run my hand along the edge of the lid, as Mother once did on another coffin, but this one is a very simple and cheap one. ('Don't worry about that,' she would say. 'It doesn't matter in the least.') Talking to Jaime was a necessary respite, and now I am confronting this grief again. The tears gush out with a violence that still surprises me. It is the coffin, of course, here under my hand, but it is the extreme kindness of the people at the Embassy, too. They are very different causes, but they are having the same effect.

My mother rested her hand on that other coffin in the undertaker's store room. His wares were all in various sober shades and made of different kinds and qualities of wood. Fern chose a fine mahogany casket for her father. He had been a skilful cabinetmaker and she wanted to bury him in good-quality wood with neat corners. She stroked the curve of the lid. 'Dad would have liked this,' she had said. We are still so involved with the dead when they are newly dead; we are their proxies when we arrange their funerals. (Is this all right? Do you like this? How am I doing?) But my hand is not her hand, because mine cannot pluck arpeggios out of strips of ivory or bow a fiddle or flick organ stops during a half rest. It's slightly smaller, too. She could reach two keys over an octave and I can't. I stroke the cheap reddish pine which will soon give up its contents and be used again.

After a time I sense the funeral men behind me getting impatient, but I am not intimidated by hearing them shift their weight from one foot to the other. They can fidget all they want. This time we are doing it my way, and it is going to take a little longer. It is going to take until I decide that we can move on.

Fern said to me once when I was still in my teens, 'I don't care what you do with my body after I'm dead. I'll be through with it.' I shuddered then at the thought of having to do anything with it. I put this episode in the distant future, well out of sight, so far in the future that different people would be involved, not me. But you can never put your life *that* far in the future, and here I am, more capable of this than I would have been as a teenager, but still not what you would call on top of it.

At length I turn around and nod to the funeral director and his pallbearers. They carry the coffin to the marble table in front of the curtain. As the coffin is being lifted from the trestle I sense extra people standing behind me. I hear women's voices and I catch the word *alma*, 'soul'.

'What are they saying behind us?' I ask Jaime, and he translates, 'God give peace to her soul.' It is uncanny that I should find another chorus of comforters, like the hotel maids and the women Marcus Cheke reported at the airmen's burial. These women have come to put flowers at the tombs and they have stopped out of curiosity to see what is happening at the crematorium. They have felt an immediate sympathy, and they have not stopped to ask who it is or whether they knew the deceased.

Then the coffin slides behind the curtain and out of sight. The funeral director asks me if I want to stay until the burning is finished; it will take an hour, he says, and another hour for the cooling off. I decline, feeling that this must be the first cremation he has ever organised. We arrange that he will send me the ashes in London.

Jaime has to go and attend to other business, but takes me as far as the top of the Avenida da Liberdade, and I gratefully thank him for driving me to the cemetery and staying with me there. When the car moves off, I realise that I am exactly in front of the *Diário de Notícias* building, behind which is the Hotel Valverde. I walk on down the boulevard on the mosaic esplanade, brushing away the tears, which have started again. I have to stop and sit on a bench and pull myself together. Here are these black and white tessellations going blurred and wavy, as they did seven years ago.

There are two good hours of daylight left. I must do something active. I decide to go back to the hotel and change clothes and then walk in the Alfama. I now walk briskly and with purpose across the Restauradores and down the Rua 1 de Dezembro to the Rua do Carmo and then Garrett. At the hotel I change into my corduroys and walking shoes and go back out again. I cross the Baixa, the low-lying shopping district that Pombal built, and then begin the climb up the other side, the escarpment below the Castle of São Jorge.

I come to the church of São António, where a service is in progress. This is the same St Anthony who has a magnificent basilica and shrine in Padua, but he was a Lisboan by birth, and this church stands on the supposed spot where he was born. St Anthony helps you find things you've lost.

In the main aisle a lighted display case holds the remains of another saint swathed in voluminous material. A group of old people is at the back of the side aisle chanting Hail Marys. I stand there for a moment feeling revolted by the embalmed saint in the glass sarcophagus. The air is stuffy with the odour of wax candles and I remember that I have not eaten much today. I feel slightly faint, and I do not want to fall on this stone floor. I suddenly turn and make my way back out of the church, through a throng of black-clad stooped old ladies.

Outside I see more tiny, tottery old ladies climbing the steep streets. I do not like the Alfama. The buildings all seem on the point of collapse and the shops look seedy and sinister. It is not picturesque, as the guidebook claimed. It is depressing and only a mountain goat could feel at home on these sidewalks. A cool wind is rising now in the late afternoon and the streets are in shadow. Climbing the narrow streets, I come to an open patio with a bare pergola along one side and a shallow pool in the middle. Although the streets are dark now, the low sun still hits this patio. The Tagus flows down below in the distance, beyond the red tile roofs. A few dirty children are playing on this one open expanse in the area, and at the far side I see a tourist information office. It seems to be open, so I go in.

The tourist information office is a gloomy little room with, however, a fine view from its windows over the sunset on the Tagus.

'Hello,' I say to the only occupant of the room, a woman sitting behind a big desk with cabriole legs.

'Hello,' she replies. 'The only thing in English is that map.' I see some brochures in German and some leaflets proclaiming Lisbon as 'unforgettable' in several languages not including English. 'The museums are closed on Monday,' she tells me. 'This is Monday,' she adds, 'and the museums are closed.' She looks at her watch. 'The Castle is closed now, too.'

I sit down wearily and try to forget the dead saint in the glass case and the horror of the cremation. I think, in spite of myself, of Jaime and Sheila's grisly errand. I know I am not going to cry again, but my head is still stuffy with all the crying I have already done, and my eyes must be red and swollen. I take out a tissue and blow my nose.

'You have a cold!' the woman exclaims. 'I have a cold. I have a flu. These winters are terrible. Everybody in Lisbon has a flu now.' She gestures irritably out toward the sunset on the Tagus. 'Everybody in Portugal.'

'Oh,' I say. 'That's too bad.'

'You better not stay here long or I will contage you. Flu is very contagious. My niece has it too.'

'How long have you had it?'

'A fortnight! It's this terrible weather.' She indicates the sunset.

'They say hot lemon juice is good for it.'

'Lemon juice! And orange juice. I've tried everything. I take syrup three times a day. My husband is coming for me at a quarter past six. I go home and make dinner for my husband and then I go to bed. I cough all night. It is in my bronchal.' She pats her upper chest. 'It is here in my bronchal. Last week I had a fever of 39°.'

I blow my nose again as a gesture of solidarity. The woman looks at her watch and would probably close the office early if I weren't sitting in it.

'Well, thanks,' I say, rising to leave. 'I hope you feel better soon. Good-bye.'

I walk back down to the Baixa, but taking a longer route than my ascent to the patio and the tourist office. It is the Lisbon rush hour, and the sidewalks are crowded with people hurrying home. Antiquated trams with steamed-up windows rattle past filled with people. I know I am going in the right direction as long as the streets tend downward. Dr Fernandes lives somewhere here in the Alfama in a certain *largo*. I take a short detour to find it, but I have forgotten which number his house is. It is an unremarkable little square. Why did he never write to me, the wretch?

I come out on flat ground at the stock exchange by the river, and only the cindery remains of the sunset are left. The crowd is thicker here, and for a time I am swept along with it toward the river terminal where ferries leave for Cacilhas and Barreiro and Seixal and Montijo across the Tagus. In the Praça do Comércio there are long queues waiting for buses and trams, and I walk on along the river toward the other ferry quay at the Cais do Sodré. Commuters hurry past me to the ferry and the suburban train station beyond. At the station I turn up to the right and climb the Rua do Alecrim to Chiado.

I go to the Tio Pepe near the hotel, a modest little restaurant where the specialty tonight is roast chicken. I am suddenly feeling very hungry. I am tired of all the primitive life forms on menus and it is nice to sit down and have a glass of chilled *vinho verde*. I feel a weird sense of accomplishment about today. It should have happened five or six years ago, but it has taken the combined efforts of past and present staff at the American Embassy to bring it about. And now it is over.

X

It is quiet in the street below my window because it is a holiday – Shrove Tuesday, *Mardi Gras*. Perhaps there will be a parade. I wouldn't mind some diversion. I take a bath, because in this hotel the hot water runs out by the middle of the morning. As I get some clothes out of the wardrobe, I am glad that they are sending me the ashes later in London. If they had given me the ashes after the cremation, as we had once tentatively planned, I would have them now and they would be in a box in the bottom of this wardrobe next to the suitcase.

The dining-room of the hotel recalls an earlier age of plaster swags and ornate mirrors. The walls are a light, 18th-century blue and the carpet is blood red. There are three waiters, and I always start out my Portuguese day with a *Bom dia* to them. Said morning after morning, it sounds repetitive to me, but the waiters take it good-humouredly.

I walk down to the Baixa and cross it on the Rua da Conceiçao and then begin the climb up the other side. I want to see the Castle of São Jorge and the view of the city from its ramparts. I take a different route up to the top from the streets I was on yesterday. I will go around the north flank. It seems from the map that you can get to the Castle entrance by circling around it on either side. Sometimes the streets in the Alfama turn into stairways with handrails in the middle, and you have the odd feeling that you are inside a huge building, something designed by Piranesi in a fever. Houses open directly onto these stairways, like rooms off a landing, and lines of washing hang overhead. Where other streets meet the relatively level Costa do Castelo there are amazing views down the dark alleyways and out over the red roofs of the city. When Hans Christian Andersen visited Lisbon, he described a big hotel whose cellar windows looked out over the roof of a five-storey house in the next street. That hotel could be anywhere here.

I circle around through the ancient Largo de Santa Cruz. As this area survived the earthquake of 1755, I assume that the houses, or many of their foundations, are unimaginably old. Some of these walls were here when the Moors controlled the castle or even when the Visigoths held it before them. There were already walls here in 48 AD.

Inside the battlements there is a drive where an occasional black and green taxi stops to let someone out. Families stroll here, and children dressed in their Carnival costumes. On the battlements there are cannons mounted on movable carriages, perhaps left-overs from the Peninsular War, when Lisbon was occupied by the French and General Junot lived in the Rua do Alecrim around the corner from my hotel. Now they point out over the city and people sit on them to have their pictures taken. A tangle of paper streamers is caught on one of the cannons, like something that got in the way of a children's birthday party.

I pick out as many landmarks as I can, because that is part of the game of going up onto high places. From up here the Avenida da Liberdade is more than ever like a river flowing between its banks. Green rows of trees mark the course of the Avenida up to the monument to Pombal and the green bushiness of the Edward VII Park beyond it. The Lisboans were so taken with the King of England when he visited here in 1903 that they named a very large park after him at what must have been the edge of the city in those days. Following the Avenue downstream, I can identify the monumental pillars of the Rossio and the Praça dos Restauradores. Across the 'river valley' are the ruins of the Carmo monastery, their distinctive bare ribs white against the deep blue sky. It doesn't look very high up, but it's on one of the higher points in the city, at the top of Eiffel's Santa Justa Elevator. I pick out the Elevator, too, connecting the Baixa with the Largo do Carmo. There is a walkway at the top, a bridge high up over the Rua 1 de Dezembro. There can't be many cities where you can take an elevator between one section and another. On weekdays, streams of office workers and shop assistants go to work by elevator, commuting vertically.

After I have identified all the landmarks I can, I take out my map to see if I can recognise anything else. One landmark I have overlooked is practically in the shadow of the Castle outcrop. It is marked on the map with a red cross in a red circle. It is the Hospital of São José.

I never knew where it was. I didn't even know we were being taken there that night. I learned the name of it from the death certificate. We went rushing through the dark streets with the siren screaming, as though there were any other traffic, as though we needed to hurry. Some of the streets were cobbled; there were sharp corners and steep places. Suddenly we were at a brightly lit entrance and the ambulance men were throwing open the rear doors. I clambered out through another door and followed them, running, into the emergency department. It is hard to be sure that this building down below the Castle is really the hospital, but now I see some white ambulances crawling like termites around to a congregating place at one side where the emergency department must be. I look at it for a long time, trying to recognise something.

It is warm up here on the Castle, and I take off my heavy sweater and tie the arms around my neck, carrying it piggyback. I go inside the ruins, where there is a little park, and climb the steps to the top of the old walls. I take some pictures, out of habit, with the little camera I carry everywhere, lining up interesting archways and shadows and gnarled olive trees. One ancient tree has a large wooden plaque mounted in front of it. Using my pocket dictionary, I read:

> You who pass by and raise your arm against me,
> Before you harm me, take a good look at me.
> I am the heat of your fireside on cold winter nights.
> I am the friendly shade that you find
> When you travel under the August sun.
> And my fruit are the refreshing taste
> That quenches your thirst on the roads.
> I am the friendly roof-beam of your house, the board of your table,
> The bed in which you rest and the timber of your boat.
> I am the handle of your hoe, the door of your home,
> The wood of your cradle and even of your coffin.
> I am the bread of goodness and the flower of beauty.
> You who pass by, take a good look at me and do not harm me.

I have seen this before, in front of another old gnarled tree in another park in Lisbon. It makes the Portuguese seem kind even to their trees. (Yes, the wood of your coffins, the wood of your kitchen cabinets …)

I go back down to the Praça da Figueira on flat ground where the river of the Avenida da Liberdade flows into the delta of little streets in the Baixa. A woman is selling long balloons filled with helium and tethered to a heavy wooden crate. Now and then parents with a young Zorro or pink fairy go past and buy one of her balloons, tying it carefully to the child's wrist or a button. There are yellow and green balloons with faces on them, blue and pink ones shaped like rabbits with long transparent ears. Crowds of people mill around in this Praça and the short streets connecting it with the nearby Rossio.

The question Lisbon puts to me – with all its ambulances, its mosaic paving, São José under the Castle, Pombal sighting down the Avenida at the Tagus – is how and when can we think again with pleasure of people who have died? Their going is painful to us, but their lives delighted us. How long does it take to forget the one and remember only the other? Or if not to forget, to get in perspective? Even when you think you've forgotten the painful part, it flares up again like a quartan in the soul. But there was more to her life than her death. Twenty minutes at the end doesn't cancel the rest. When can I have my mother back?

I find a place for lunch and order some grilled squid. The squid is good, but I am losing my enthusiasm for seafood. I am losing my enthusiasm for most things. I have no enthusiasm for Carnival. Somebody threw an egg at me a few days ago as I was walking along the Estrada Marginal, the fast highway alongside the Tagus. He was riding pillion on a motorcycle and hit me squarely in the small of my back, and the egg felt as hard as a baseball. It seemed an unnecessarily nasty thing to do to an innocent stranger walking along the road. You're in town for your mother's cremation wearing a suede coat that you want to look presentable at the cemetery the next day, and someone hits you with a 50-mph egg. What kind of heartless monsters inhabit this place, anyway? I curtailed my walk at the next train station and went straight back to the hotel, holding the coat gingerly across my arms to keep the egg from running any more than it had already. Back in my hotel room, I poured full-strength liquid detergent on the egg to break up the fat and mopped the mess off the suede. It dried a bit stiff and I had missed a few spatters, but the coat was wearable. I'm still a bit jittery about traffic coming from behind me, though.

This must be the way Fern felt all the time. She never liked to hear car engines behind her. I only gradually became aware of her discomfort as a pedestrian, especially in Britain, where the traffic was on the wrong side of the street anyway. Even more gradually it dawned on me that the reason for this uneasiness was the Accident. The cars that hit her had come from behind and one side, crashing together at right angles and then slewing into her. Then I noticed that a fleeting expression of alarm nearly always crossed her face when she heard squealing brakes, even if she was indoors at the time. That moment in August 1938 on a street corner in Chicago was always with her and could be recalled in an instant by certain sounds.

I see broken eggs on the sidewalk from time to time, and once in the Largo do Carmo, where there is a school, I found some children throwing eggs at each other. This practice must have some relevance to Shrove Tuesday, but it seems pointless and wasteful, to say nothing of the effect it has on a suede coat and one's nerves.

The squid is on a bed of rice. Fern would no doubt have liked this. She enjoyed seafood, perhaps because we didn't have much of it in Indiana. When we drove east, eating at Howard Johnson's restaurants along the way, we would get to a place where fried clams were on the menu and then we knew we were out of the Midwest. She would try any interesting new food. This memory gives me no pleasure now, although I feel it somehow should. It only brings twinges of grief.

Carnival in Lisbon seems to be a day of making *paseos*, of seeing and being seen. Near the Praça de Figueira I see a family of four clowns getting out of their car and arranging their masks and costumes before making their appearance before the public. A big clown stoops over to help a very small clown with the blouse of its outfit and then all four set out to add to the festive crowds. The crowds are, however, mostly in civvies, and the clowns, Zorros, and pink fairies are in the minority, like people on their way to a costume party. This party has been going on for the past week, by all appearances, as the guests have been in transit in the streets of Lisbon for all that time.

I do not honestly know quite why I want to go and look at

the São José Hospital. Perhaps I want to see if I recognise anything. I want to look at it in daylight. I go along the Rua da Palma and up a flight of steps to a higher road. There's a pink outer wall with a gate in it and an inner yard, but no sign anywhere identifying the hospital. Our ambulance would have come from the other direction. I wander around to the right side of the building, where I saw the ambulances from the Castle battlements. A white ambulance is sitting at the entrance with a taxi behind it. A little knot of anxious-looking people has formed at the doorway. I do not remember such a narrow passage between the hospital and that high wall. I do not remember this entrance. Nothing at all looks familiar. I have no memory of how we got back to the hotel, except that the cardiologist must have taken us in his car. We were at the hospital with him and then we were back at the hotel with him. There must be some other emergency entrance where we went that night. It may be on another side of this large building or complex of buildings. I suddenly do not want to look for it. Suppose I found it? What difference would it make?

I walk north along the Rua da Palma. The air is cooler now and a wind is getting up. The Rua da Palma is like another river valley, running into the same delta as the Avenida da Liberdade. The Metro line runs under both these avenues, making a big V shape. I pass a tram stop named after a Christian who fell fighting the Moors for the Castle in 1147. Immortality takes many forms. The Laura Alves Theatre is showing a musical review called *Our Love is Lisbon* and the pictures outside the theatre show sets made to look like the narrow streets of the Alfama, with street lamps on brackets fastened to the houses.

As elsewhere in Lisbon, here on the Avenida da Palma there is a mixture of very shabby buildings and recently painted ones. There are balconies everywhere. Childish laughter is coming from one of them. I look up and see some children on a be-streamered balcony four floors up joyously flinging confetti into the air. It rains down at an angle because of the stiff breeze. I suppose it's catching in my hair. Anyway, they're not throwing eggs.

As I go on up the Rua da Palma and the Avenida Almirante Reis past the Metro stations, I do not know it, but I am actually following the course of a prehistoric river. The Avenida da Liberdade, which flows like a river between its steep banks, was also once a prehistoric river. The delta of narrow shopping streets built by Pombal after the catastrophe of 1755 was once a real delta where the ancient tributaries met the ancient Tagus. The commuters of this busy capital follow the same route as their predecessors of 10,000 years ago as they speared fish from dugout canoes.

If the cardiologist summoned by the hotel and the ambulance sent by the fire brigade had arrived earlier, could they have saved her? The Portuguese cardiologist thought not. The doctor in Plainfield also thought not. 'A massive heart attack like that,' he said. 'Nothing could have saved her, probably.' I was talking to him over dinner, describing in detail what had so recently happened and probably ruining the appetites of all the other dinner guests. 'No,' he said, 'it sounds like she wouldn't have survived it even if you'd gotten her to the hospital right away.' But was he saying that just to make me feel better? Is it a routine part of his job to reassure people that they have not been negligent when death slips through their defences?

I stop in a little café full of Zorros and pink fairies and their parents to have a cup of coffee and a pastry. The children are being treated to ice cream, and some of the little Zorros have white moustaches from it. One little boy is sitting with an older woman who I think must be his grandmother. I watch them together and try to figure out their relationship. A younger woman is with them, but she is not his mother. An aunt, possibly.

During the year after Fern died I would sometimes have dreams that denied her death. We would meet unexpectedly and I would say brightly, 'Oh, you're not dead after all!' She would explain that it had all been a mistake; there was some other explanation for what had happened. No, she had not died in Lisbon; she had revived and now here we were, meeting again. The grief that I felt then, even asleep, would disappear, and we would laugh at the foolish misunderstanding. Then I would wake up and realise what my unconscious mind was up to. Nice try, I would tell it, but it won't work.

I wonder if I have confetti in my hair. If so, it is a kind of badge for today of being part of the people around me. We are all hilarious merry-makers together. Whoopee, Carnival. Whoopee, confetti and streamers. Whoopee, broken eggs and funny outfits.

It's getting chilly and the evening is settling into the streets. At the next Metro station, I go down into the corridors built on the old river bed and take the train to the Rossio. It's almost dark now, and the balloon-sellers have gone home. Carnival seems to be over. In the *Diário de Notícias* the next day, I read that most people in Portugal, except for certain places with particular traditions, just had a day off to relax. In some towns there were parades and floats. At Mealhada a television actor was the King of the Carnival, and at Torres Vedras there were crowds in the streets, and some entertainers in doublets and hose added to the festivities. There is a big picture of the street entertainers on the front page, and at the bottom of the page a photograph of one of the principal streets in Lisbon, almost deserted. The caption says that most Lisboans preferred to celebrate Carnival by sleeping late.

Tomorrow is Ash Wednesday. I do my best not to dwell on any ironic associations.

As I am walking up the Rua Garrett – at the spot where the man had an epileptic fit – I hit on an idea. I have been trying to find a way of avoiding being served fish with the head on. At the Tio Pepe and at other restaurants, I keep ordering the kinds of fish that are prepared in this way. Now I hit on the solution to the problem. I will always ask for a big fish so that they *can't* bring me the whole thing! This idea should have been obvious, but it has taken me a lot of meals with fish heads to think of it.

At the hotel, grouper is on the menu for tonight. I think I have seen a picture of a grouper somewhere, and it was a big, ugly fish, so I plan to have my evening meal at the hotel. Tonight they will serve a cross-section of the fish, a 'steak', and so what appears on my plate will not even be fish-shaped.

In the hotel dining-room I am given the menu and the waiter hovers at my side while I look at it. '*Está bem*,' I say and hand the menu back to him. I am the only one in the vast dining-room at this hour and at this time of year. Some mediocre soup arrives. I could make better soup than this. Anybody could. They have really not got the knack in this hotel kitchen. Their cooking doesn't match the décor. You might expect something rather grand on the table to match the plaster swags and mouldings on the walls. Overhead there are glass chandeliers the size and shape of Christmas trees.

My main course arrives. This is the test of my new plan to avoid being served the whole fish with the head attached, and the plan certainly seems foolproof. However, there is one possibility I have not considered. What comes on the platter from the kitchen and is served onto my plate is a large boiled fish head. It has sickening flat eyes and horrible boiled lips. Do people eat fish heads? There can't be much meat on this one. Some sharp little teeth are visible through the slightly parted boiled lips.

One of the waiters I know from breakfast asks me if it is all right. Is he kidding? A fish head? The *head* of a fish? What do they take me for? No wonder this dining-room is usually empty. '*Não*,' I say, and then I forget all the Portuguese words I learned from the Berlitz tape. I tell him in Spanish that I would rather have a different piece of the fish. Another waiter comes along and enquires about my meal and I summon some Portuguese. '*Não a cabeça*,' I say weakly – not the head – '*por favor*.' I glance down at the unspeakable boiled lips on my plate.

There is a short argument among the breakfast waiter and the other one and the head waiter, and they all three sweep back into the kitchen with my plate. Can they be serious? Is it supposed to be some kind of delicacy? This wouldn't happen at the Rio Vinho, where the fish didn't even have bones, never mind heads. Are they doing this for a bet? Am I on Candid Camera?

I admit that I don't know much about fish – I rarely eat it unless I'm someplace where it's supposed to be a local specialty – and perhaps it's merely naive to be revolted by a fish head, but I suspect that it is not. When it comes to fish, the most knowledgeable person I know is my Scottish mother-in-law. She grew up in a fishing port and has a very professional eye about anything with scales. No fishmonger or restaurateur has ever put anything over on her. And *she* doesn't like fish heads either! She would send this object back to the kitchen, too. ('Och lassie, for goodness' *sake*!')

The waiters all emerge from the kitchen with another platter. Now they serve me the tail. There is the caudal fin of the animal and some grey flesh at the base of it.

'Is this all right?' the breakfast waiter asks. 'The rest of the fish is gone.'

I don't want to look for another restaurant now. 'Yes, it's all right,' I say. But where can it have gone, I wonder. There aren't enough people staying in this hotel to eat a large fish, and the smart ones don't eat here anyway.

The fish is merely boiled without any kind of garnish or sauce. My mother-in-law would have done something much more creative with it. The fishermen should have left this creature where they found it. Afterwards I go to the hotel bar for a cup of coffee to get rid of the taste, if not the memory, of the fish, but the bar is closed because of Carnival. I then go next door to the Brasileira, which specialises in coffee and is open. My mouth finally tastes of fine Brazilian coffee, but my mind still harbours the wretched grouper.

I see in the *Diário de Notícias* that there is some sort of trouble in Timor, the island the Portuguese found 470-odd years ago. They may have put fear on the map, but they didn't discover it. *Timor mortis conturbat me*. Nor is it only East Timor: it is in every direction.

XI

I walk past the music shop with all the stringed instruments in the window – lutes and ukuleles and round, blond fado guitars. I cross the Praça Luís Camões, which is built on a slope with steps at one end. I am on my way to the Museum of Ancient Art in a street called Green Windows. Gaziel, a Spanish visitor to Lisbon, writes in *Far-away Portugal*, 'Maps of Lisbon, so as not to be misleading, should have elevation markings and contour lines, like Geological Survey maps.' The mistaken impression consists in this, he goes on: the map is two dimensional, but when you walk through Lisbon you are faced with gradients ranging from a gentle incline to an abrupt ascent or a vertiginous descent. What looks like three steps on the map, he says, turns into three thousand because there is a deep valley in the way. I go in a fairly direct line to the museum in the Street of the Green Windows, but it means skirting the southern part of the Bairro Alto and traversing streets that turn into stairs, as in the Alfama. One steep, narrow street has a tramline down the middle of it, and I recall that Lisbon has the steepest tramlines in the world. Front doors of houses open directly onto this street; the residents must look both ways for trams before putting a foot outside their door.

The 'Ancient Art' turns out to be mostly medieval and Renaissance. There are ceramics, furniture and carpets, but the paintings are the most interesting. These religious paintings of the 15th and 16th centuries certainly wouldn't convert an outsider to Christianity. The images are ugly and repellent.

There are morbid scenes of martyrdoms and hell. There are some saints and Annunciations, but nobody looks very happy. There is a lot of death about: dead and dying saints, Descents from the Cross, Entombments. A person coming to Christianity from some other scheme of things would not care to take part in any of these activities. But then, the Church wasn't in the evangelical business in those days; rather it was apparently in the business of maintaining its power by scaring the socks off people.

A certain morbidity is inevitable in medieval Christianity. Perhaps it's a mistake to see so much of this together. In the Middle Ages most people would not have seen walls covered with so many paintings all in the same place. They would not have had a lifetime total of a thousand and one St Sebastians. There is a sameness in the figures and their reverence or misery, depending on the situation. Actual human, earthly, enjoyment doesn't count for much. Even the artists themselves don't seem to have enjoyed their senses. But who am I to blame them for being morbid?

> When I shall die I know no day,
> What country or place I cannot say:
> Wherefore this song sing I may –
> *Timor mortis conturbat me*.

From the morbidity of the paintings I turn to the museum itself. It is an old *palácio* in which Pombal is said to have been born. At any rate, it was his family's town residence. Now it is a rather severe-looking building painted pale ochre and white on the outside. Inside it is a beautifully designed museum of art. There are spotlights and dark walls; the floors are marble or polished wood; and the stairways are so modern that Pombal would scarcely have recognised them as stairways.

The sky is a vivid blue today, and the yellow and white of the outside walls is so bright that it hurts my eyes. The harbour and the coastal road are down a long flight of steps to the south. It is too warm for a coat today, and I am wearing a large woollen scarf tied loosely around my shoulders. I bought it in a little hole-in-the-wall shop where I saw it hanging outside by the door. I was so taken by its brown and green pattern that I crossed the street to have a better look. The woman who ran the shop was busy talking to three friends at the counter, and I felt shy about interrupting them. I had momentarily forgotten the word for either 'scarf' or 'shawl' and I wasn't sure what I was going to say. The fewer in my audience the better, but now all four of them turned an expectant gaze on me. 'Excuse me,' I said, 'how much is this?' The proprietress came out from behind the counter and told me the price of the one I had asked about and showed me some other similar ones. I chose the one that had originally caught my eye and she put it in a bag for me. She and her three friends seemed so friendly that I asked where the scarf was from.

From the North, they said, Trás-os-Montes, up around there. Not from around here, not from Lisbon.

'It's very pretty,' I said.

Yes, they said, very pretty, but from the North.

Their manner was so pleasant that, although the transaction was banal in the extreme, it left me with a good feeling. The women and I had made friendly sounds to each other and I had come away with my scarf.

Now, outside the Museum of Ancient Art, I retie it loosely at my collar. I wander along the river almost as far as Alcântara and the big bridge of 25 April, named after the date of the *coup* of 1974. Before that it was called the Salazar Bridge. At one restaurant I see a truck unloading huge crates of dried cod imported from Norway. Dried cod fish is a staple of every kitchen in Portugal, and they import it from Norway! The Tagus, presumably full of fish, if not many of them cod, is in sight, and they import dried fish from Norway. The men unloading the crates don't seem to find anything unusual about ‘Norway’ being written all over them, but I am mystified as I watch them.

On sunny days like this I am on the lookout for things to take pictures of – things and angles and light. On the Street of the Green Windows there is some sort of official building with an unattended door on the street. Inside there is a small vestibule and then a flight of stone steps up to the left. I glance past the wrought-iron gate and see a Swiss-cheese plant in an old clay pot. The light coming through the iron grille casts interesting shadows of the grille and the Swiss-cheese plant onto the white stone wall. On an impulse I step inside, go up a few steps, and arrange the plant and its complex shadows in my viewfinder. I hope there is enough light for my uncomplicated little camera. I think there is. I’ll risk it.

I buy some postcards at a little shop where I am the only customer. When I pay for them, the woman behind the counter warns me about bag-snatchers. She seems both solemn and protective, and I thank her and tell her I will be careful. Can Lisbon be so dangerous? It doesn’t look very dangerous in broad daylight, but still I carry my bag with the buckle turned inward to foil pickpockets and I keep a good grip on the strap. But I do this anyway in London.

Lisbon is full of pleasant distractions, but I can’t will myself to feel enjoyment. It is a desperate last resort to think, ‘But *she* would have wanted me to enjoy myself.’ This leads to absurdity, because you can’t take pleasure in something just to please someone else, especially one who is not present or even alive. Can you cajole yourself into feeling happy for someone else’s benefit? I doubt it. It is pleasant enough to stroll around the city and buy scarves and admire the look of the place, but I often remember my mother and the fun goes out of things. Considering that I have spent a negligible part of my life in Lisbon, I have wept inordinately here. Some of the mosaic pavements have wavy patterns – in the Rossio they are supposed to symbolise the tidal wave after the earthquake – but I have often seen them wavy with tears.

I knew my mother well enough to know what she would say on most occasions and how she would say it. Even now I can imagine her telling me to snap out of it. She would say,'Well, my dear, we don't live for ever. People die, and the living have to go on with their lives.' It's like being reminded of the key signature from another room. I don't think she was afraid of death. When she was about to die, she said to me, 'If this is a heart attack, that's all right.' The horror of that night comes back and I remember how she slipped through my fingers before the ambulance arrived. But she didn't seem to mind; she minded less than I did.

Once when I was about six I was visiting one of our lodgers in her room upstairs in the Old Brick House in Danville, and she began to tell me how a dead body is prepared by an undertaker. 'They drain the blood out at the wrists, here,' she said, showing me on her wrists where it was done. 'Then they pump embalming fluid into the veins. They put little patches over the places, and that's why you never see the wrists of the dead person in the casket.'

Horrified, I ran down the winding staircase past all the little hunting scenes to my mother and sobbed in her lap that Jean had told me how the blood was drained out of dead people. Interrupted in the middle of some mending, Fern suddenly had to deal with this unexpected situation which had fallen literally in her lap. I think of her sitting on the edge of the bed concentrating on the hem she was stitching, and perhaps pondering at the same time the tree that was going to have to come down or the gas bill. Anyway, not the question of embalming the dead. I imagine her quickly moving the needles and scissor points out of the way of the small frightened girl now burrowing into her lap.

She stroked my hair and told me that it didn't matter greatly what happened to a dead body once the spirit had left it. Did I remember that butterfly cocoon we found? The butterfly wouldn't have cared what happened to it, would it?

A person's body was like that cocoon. Once you're through with your body you don't care what happens to it. So the blood doesn't really matter one way or the other, does it?

Gradually I stopped whimpering. 'She shouldn't have told you that,' my mother said. (I think I can remember the severity in her voice. Before long Jean probably heard it, too.) 'But it's not really frightening, is it?' Now her voice was soothing. 'It doesn't matter to the person who's finished with his body, does it?' The horror I had felt was slowly evaporating. It was no more horrible than a butterfly's cast-off cocoon. But I still didn't like to think about it.

'A certain amount of grief is normal, of course,' she would tell me now. 'You'll get over it,' she would say confidently.

The craft and souvenir shop is positioned just where several narrow alleyways widen into a *largo* in the Alfama. A young woman, perhaps still in her teens, is standing behind the counter chatting to an older woman.

'Hello,' she says cheerfully in English. 'Can I help you?'

'Could I see some filigree pins, please?'

'Yes, of course,' she says, coming from behind the counter. She goes to a glass display case and takes out a tray of silver-gilt brooches. They represent delicate leaves of various shapes and sizes. They are all made with great skill and I look closely at several of them. I have decided to buy one as a treat for myself. It is going to be a special souvenir of this time and place, and in the short term it is going to make the time and place more bearable. As I look at them and compare the prices and ponder my choice, the saleswoman continues her conversation with the older woman, who I surmise is a neighbour.

'They all take so long to make up their minds!' the older woman exclaims in Portuguese. 'I wouldn't have the patience!'

'Oh, but I have plenty of time and I don't mind,' the

saleswoman replies placidly.

I feel mild annoyance with the older woman and a corresponding warmth toward the saleswoman. I shall definitely buy one of her brooches!

'How do they make them?' I ask.

'They start with a thin piece of silver and then with a tiny pin they make holes in it. When they're finished they dip it in a gold bath.'

I finally choose a little brooch in the shape of a narrow leaf like the leaf of an olive tree that curves in a shallow, graceful S.

'Thanks very much,' I say when she hands me my leaf in a little envelope. 'And thanks for being so patient. I took a long time to decide.'

'That's all right,' she laughs, making a little wave of her hand. 'It's no trouble.'

In a little shop in the Baixa I buy on impulse a small alabaster pot with a hinged lid. It is scarcely a suitable souvenir of Lisbon, as it says clearly on it in English that it was made in Italy, but I have taken a fancy to it. Anyway, I'm having an interesting, and unusually successful, conversation in my hybrid Hispano-Portuguese with the two women behind the counter. I pay for the alabaster pot and am given it wrapped up like a gift. As I put it in my shoulder bag, one of the women says, 'Be careful with your bag. There are a lot of thieves about.'

'I am careful, but thanks for the warning,' I say. 'How do you carry your bag? Like this?' I indicate my bag with the buckle turned inward.

'Yes, that's best,' one of them says. 'The streets aren't so dangerous now, during the day, but it's different at night.'

'And in the Metro,' says the second woman. 'You have to be very careful in the Metro. The trains and buses, too, but the Metro is the worst place.'

'I've never had my bag stolen,' the first woman remarks.

'No,' says her colleague, 'I've never had my bag stolen, either.'

'My wallet was stolen once in Madrid,' I say.

'Ah, Madrid,' one of them says, nodding. 'You have to be careful everywhere.'

I wonder if there is really a crime wave in Lisbon, or is it a kind of myth that is spread by rumour and these frequent warnings?

The grief comes back like twinges of rheumatism in wet weather. Mother hadn't reached 80. After she died people said to me, in an effort to look on the bright side, 'But she was a good age.' I could only think that she might have been a still better age; she might have lived for another 10 years, say. When she died at 78, I was 37. I thought, 'Seventy-eight – is that all?' but I also meant, 'Thirty-seven – is that all?' Her mother was 87 when she died. Was that too much to expect? She had an aunt who lived to 102, so something well into the 80s didn't seem unreasonable. However, by now she would have been well into her 80s.

People also kept telling me seven years ago that it was good that I had been with her and that she had died quickly and painlessly. Her contemporaries whom I met later in Plainfield stressed these points. They all came up with the same three or four clichés. They clearly identified more with the elderly mother than with the daughter in her 30s. Oh, she died quickly all right, and yes indeed, I had been with her. I could understand, with some effort, that these had been preferable to other possible circumstances. These assurances sounded suspiciously glib, but thoughtful and intelligent old ladies in their 70s and 80s have lived too long to be merely glib, and what they say bears considering. The clichés that I heard so often were true. In the end I was grateful to her friends for helping me to see the situation from their, and therefore my mother's, point of view.

When I look at menus outside restaurants I think of the horrible grouper with its grey, cooked lips. My appetite is still on vacation. At least in Portugal you can't go wrong with the coffee. Fern drank her coffee so hot that it was just off the boil. In any restaurant she ever went into anywhere, one of her main objects was to get really hot coffee. 'I'd like *hot* coffee,' she would say to the waitress, hoping that the extra emphasis would help. I never knew how she drank it. Sometimes the coffee that came was hot enough, and then she would have to take the first few sips from a teaspoon because it was too hot for even her to drink in the normal way. I, naturally, waited for my own coffee to cool off enough to be drinkable. After it had cooled for 10 or 15 minutes, she would enquire innocently, 'Are you waiting for ice to form around the edges?' Her insistence on hot coffee was a running joke with everyone she had ever dined with.

In the evening I eat some fruit I have kept in my hotel room and listen to fado music on my walkman, and I browse through the *Diário de Notícias*. East Timor is now closed to foreigners and the last Portuguese official has left. The United Nations is expected to look into the situation; refugees report the use of torture. What the newspaper fails to tell me is that Timor wasn't named by the Portuguese after all. It was already called Timor when they got there and means simply 'East' in one of the languages spoken on the island. (But if you live in a place, surely it's not 'east', but 'here'. The Land of the Rising Sun is only that to the people living to the west of it. It seems odd to name one's home according to the way strangers see it.) So I was wrong and *Timor* is a native Spice Islands word; it is not *timor*, *timoris*, a third declension masculine noun.

Before I go to bed I drape my brown and green scarf over the hotel's suit stand so that I can admire it from a distance and see the whole pattern.

XII

The Cervejaria da Trindade is a wonderful old cavernous restaurant. I like it as soon as I step inside. I like the tiles all over the walls and the pictures painted on the tiles of 17th-century Portuguese cavaliers. The Cervejaria da Trindade must seat hundreds of people, but it feels cosy in spite of its size. They have good shellfish and they make perfect omelettes. (It goes without saying that they know how to serve fish.) I have been looking for a suitable place to have a little luncheon party, and this is it. It is a popular restaurant and in the evenings it usually echoes agreeably with diners sharing jokes and enjoying themselves. The waiters are quick and friendly, and there is even a newspaper kiosk in the middle of it.

I have been in Lisbon long enough to regret having to leave it. It's that odd anticipated homesickness: I know that I'll miss it in the future and that makes me miss it now, even though I'm still here. Perhaps I'm catching *saudade*. I'll miss the Cervejaria da Trindade and its cheerful atmosphere. I'll regret never having made it to the Naval Museum or the Madre de Deus Church. I'll miss the Tagus and the black and white mosaic paving. The thought that I won't be here this time next week makes me all the more attentive to my surroundings.

The Portuguese language hangs in the air. It would be fatiguing to have to negotiate one's whole life in a foreign language, but for a tourist it is a toy. Spanish is my point of reference, and I notice that the Spanish *h* and *j* become *f* and *lh* in Portuguese. (Or rather, the medieval Spanish *f* remains in Portuguese, having changed to *h* in modern Spanish.) The *b* becomes *v*, and the *l* turns into *r*. In Spanish stem-changing verbs, diphthongs like *ie* and *ue* remain *e* and *o* in Portuguese. The Spanish *ñ* is simply *n* in Portuguese. William J. Entwhistle, describing the Portuguese language, observes, 'The loss of *l* and *n* has brought together so many vowels that Portuguese is more vocalic than any language nearer than Polynesia.' It certainly sounds nothing like Spanish, in spite of the visual similarity. If anything, it sounds to me like Polish. I find all this intriguing, and I play with it by reading public notices and newspapers and trying to speak to waiters and shopkeepers. If I had to deal with anything more serious I could not have such an amateurish attitude. What holds Europe together isn't so much the Common Market, I realise, as the Latin language and its daughters, otherwise how could I make sense of these stories in the *Diário de Notícias*? The outcome of a football match causes such a *sensação* that it's on the front page. Portuguese at this level is a puzzle that is hard enough to be interesting but not hard enough to be discouraging.

At the Gulbenkian Museum the various works of European fine and applied art are labelled in Portuguese, and it seems to me terribly European to find French Belle-Epoque furniture or Flemish Old Masters described in Portuguese. It makes me feel extremely trans-Atlantic. At least there is a drawing by Mary Cassatt representing my hemisphere.

The gloom inside the Gulbenkian Foundation – the better for preserving the colours of the paintings and textiles – is almost matched by the dull skies outside it. Behind the Museum is a large landscaped park with little waterways and an amphitheatre. The trees drip under a grey sky and the air is damp and cold. There are several Dutch and Flemish paintings and some by Fragonard and Watteau. And Rubens. This can't be the best Rubens could do. A picture of two pairs of amorous centaurs goes wrong somewhere in the anatomy and there are not enough legs to go around. Four centaurs have sixteen legs; they can't have been easy to paint, and Rubens has managed only fifteen, as far as I can see. I pause for a while and try to find the missing leg. Perhaps Rubens needed to have a model standing before him to get the legs to come out even, and centaurs being thin on the ground at the Antwerp zoo, he simply miscalculated. Maybe he got tired of painting centaur legs by the time he got to fifteen and thought that would be enough to give the idea, never imagining that anyone would be so literal-minded as to count them. There is a nice portrait of Helena Fourment, though. She presumably *was* standing in front of him. (Her legs are covered, but she undoubtedly has the right number.)

The Gulbenkian Museum is beyond the Parque Eduardo VII and so is on one of my pendulum swings to the north. I usually take the Metro to the farthest point of my explorations and then walk back. These trips through the city give me a feel for the map, and in the evening I trace my walks of that day and plan new ones for the next day. I've covered most of the Metro system and I've walked great distances along the main thoroughfares and through the steep, winding alleys of the older quarters. I have not seen all of Lisbon with the thoroughness I would wish, but I have begun to feel that I somehow 'know' it now. I feel about Lisbon the sort of affection and possessiveness that people feel about the place where they went to college or spent their honeymoon.

As it's raining, I get on a tram, an *eléctrico*. I sit behind the compartment where the driver stands and watch him operate the windshield wiper. There is a lever inside to operate the wiper on the outside, out in the rain. The driver gives the windshield a wipe from time to time when the visibility sinks to zero. We go all the way out to Alcântara and turn around and come back. If the driver can't see any better than I can, it's a good thing we're on tracks.

The Rossio has always been an open space. It has been a

cattle market, a place for burning heretics at the stake, and a place for plotting the overthrow of monarchies and dictators. After a busy day of burning heretics, the square would be covered in ashes, which were then swept up and thrown into the Tagus. When Pombal rebuilt the city, he left this old square as it had been. Now the National Theatre is at one end and two big fountains plash amid the traffic. This sidewalk café, The Pic-nic, has an enclosed patch of the sidewalk so that you can pretend that you are taking the air even when the damp Atlantic winds are dumping buckets of rain on Lisbon.

I scuttle through the rain from the tram stop to The Pic-nic and slide through the plastic flap to the enclosed terrace. I find an empty corner table and order Nescafé (which is the Portuguese for decaffeinated coffee) and hot milk with a croissant. To one side, the National Theatre and the column of Pedro IV are a vivid red owing to the red glass folding partition protecting me from the elements. As the front of the terrace is screened by cloudy-clear plastic, the rest of the Rossio is foggy but coloured normally. If I look from the lurid north side of the Rossio to the normal south side, the cream-coloured range of buildings on the south looks oddly drab, brightening gradually as I gaze at it. Then if I glance back to the north, the National Theatre and one of the fountains seem to be on fire. The dual vision is distracting. They contradict each other, and neither one is reality.

Fine old cities with a romantic and varied past fascinate me. Fern must have felt something like this about Chicago, although its past is negligible compared to that of European capitals. She liked it so much that we used to listen to Chicago radio stations instead of the much nearer Indianapolis ones when we were getting ready in the morning to go out to the hamlet my grandfather called 'New Chin-whiskers'.

Although Fern had not been personally acquainted with Al Capone (I asked her once) her Chicago was still a dangerous and exciting place. At one rooming house where she stayed there was a break-in and robbery. The police came and measured the footprints and examined the forced window. The upshot was that it had been an inside job. The landlady had let the burglar in and together they had damaged the window and positioned the footprints to mislead the police. That was the kind of thing that happened in Chicago. The Accident was another feature of Chicago, that city of the exotic, the sinister, and the plain peculiar. One of the drivers was Chinese, the other being an uninsured insurance salesman. In spite of the Accident, Fern still liked Chicago. She liked Carl Sandburg's poem about Chicago:

> Hog Butcher for the World,
> Tool Maker, Stacker of Wheat,
> Player with the Railroads and the Nation's Freight Handler;
> Stormy, husky, brawling,
> City of the Big Shoulders …

She used to say that her secret ambition was to drive a fire engine down State Street in the rush hour.

I suppose it represented bright lights to her as a young woman, and she always revered the University of Chicago, where she had heard Gertrude Stein and Eugene O'Neill lecture. I can understand how it is possible to have a special feeling of fondness for a city in spite of unpleasant experiences in it. The two things seem to be separate, so that the bad experiences do not cast a negative pall over the whole city. Perhaps they even intensify one's response to it. So Lisbon or Lisboa, the city on seven or nine or eleven hills by the Tejo or Tagus, with the Elevator by Eiffel or Mesnier, founded by Ulysses or the Romans or the Phoenicians, exercises its charm on me, although by rights I should hate the place.

I am in a shop up near the Pombal circle that is a real tourist trap, but a nice one. I want to be sure I'm not missing any good fado tapes. An enthusiastic young man in the shop speaks English and is only too happy to help me buy things.

'Who is the best fado singer? Amália Rodrigues?' I ask.

'She was the best,' he tells me, 'but she doesn't sing any more.'

'Who's the best now?'

'Oh, Maria da Fé!' he answers, beaming as though he were engaged to her. 'Maria da Fé is the best!'

'What about guitar music? I like the Portuguese guitar very much.'

'Jaime Santos is the best guitarist,' he says, plucking tape cassettes from the rack.

I look at the other souvenirs – pottery, leather goods, filigree gold and silver, and hundreds of colourful chickens representing the Cock of Barcelos, the national symbol – but it's music I want to take home with me. I already have a little stack of tape cassettes on my dresser at the hotel. I will listen to the *fadistas* in London and think of the palm trees and blue skies of Lisbon. I will think of the restaurants with choreographed waiters and women in black shawls singing in a little semi-circle of guitarists.

Now that I have met some Portuguese people, it is easier to believe Camoens' description of the sailors under Vasco da Gama. Camoens portrays them as decent family men, patriotic and deeply religious. They seem a bit too kindly and virtuous to be 16th-century adventurers, but yet when Magellan's men stopped in Rio de Janeiro in 1519 before circumnavigating the world, the locals didn't want them to leave and followed them out to sea, begging them to come back. Before the war, Philip S. Marden wrote in *A Wayfarer in Portugal*: 'The prevailing character of the people is that of sobriety, industry and kindliness. One is certain to be impressed in especial manner by the uniform courtesy and good nature shown, the helpfulness of even the humblest and the manifest desire to please … in the main it is safe to say anyone who goes thither will unfeignedly like the Portuguese.' It sounds like an exaggeration, and I always doubt such blanket generalisations, but I find it hard to disagree with this one, making allowances for certain exceptions – high-speed eggs and negligent paperwork, for example. Ann Bridges and Susan Lowndes are more succinct in their *Selective Traveller in Portugal*, where they jointly exclaim, 'When all is said and done, what a lovable people is this, and what a happy one!'

I phone the Embassy to arrange my luncheon party, but what with Carnival and Lincoln's Birthday and a weekend, it takes longer to organise than I had anticipated. Finally it is all settled, and I go to the Cervejaria da Trindade to make reservations with a waiter I have come to know. I look forward to talking with the Embassy people about something different, something ordinary. I welcome the chance to talk about anything besides the topic that has filled my letters and telephone calls to the Embassy for the past few years.

Out at the Museum of the City of Lisbon at the far end of Campo Grande, I am looking at the collection of Luso-Roman funerary pots for ashes. These pots were found on the site of the ancient Luso-Roman cemetery under the Praça da Figueira. For archaeologists death is one of the signs of life. There are a lot of Roman gravestones, and another room is full of medieval headstones with crosses carved on them.

I took Fern to the British Museum once when she was visiting me in London. When we got to the Egyptian mummies, she said, 'Immortality! They tried so hard to deny death!' It was clear that she didn't approve of this doomed attempt. It was very much the reaction of someone who was beginning to face the prospect of death and didn't need soothing rituals. I saw the Egyptian funerary customs as an expression of polytheism and sun worship; I hadn't considered the Egyptians before as real people trying to pretend that death did not exist. I think Fern found them not so much primitive – which would have been excusable in a people living 4,000 years ago – as simply wrong-headed.

Where São Jorge Castle now stands there were once temples to Jupiter and Minerva, I learn in the City Museum. The Castle itself looks old enough to antedate time, but its builders were developing a prime urban site when they demolished the temples and put up their new castle. It was Visigothic before it was Moorish. Somehow the new restaurant up there with American Express and Diners Club stickers on the door seems in keeping with the tradition of adding expressions of a newer culture to a foundation of an older one.

The City Museum is contained in an 18th-century house. Some of the original rooms are preserved, so that one walks from Roman and Visigothic artifacts into an 18th-century kitchen, past some 18th-century furniture and into an 18th-century dining-room. Upstairs Lisbon history moves along to this century with its revolutions and relatively benign dictators. Massive oil paintings depict most of Lisbon strolling in the Rossio or grouping behind barricades, depending on the politics of the moment. It is a museum inside a museum – inside yet another museum, if you include the city of Lisbon itself, which Brigid Brophy has called 'one of the most ravishing works of art in Europe'.

It was this same city, rising in tiers above the Tagus, that sent out its explorers. As they went, they left a trail of Portuguese names behind them, like scattered breadcrumbs. I used to wonder about *Formosa*, which doesn't sound at all Chinese, but of course it is the Portuguese for 'beautiful', cognate with Spanish *hermosa*. Natal was discovered on Christmas Day, and Rio de Janeiro was discovered in January. The Strait of Magellan was named after Fernão de Magalhães, and Tristan da Cunha after the man of that name, who went on an embassy to the Pope in 1514. The Portuguese towns of Lagos and Belém were commemorated in Nigeria and Brazil. Otherwise the new islands and rivers seem to have been named after the men who discovered or mapped them, the ships they sailed on, or most commonly, the name of the day in the Church calendar on which the place was discovered, like Trinidad, Ascension, St Helena, and Natal. Many of the names were superseded by later European or indigenous ones. Like breadcrumbs, those names sank into the water and appear only on very old maps.

In walking around Lisbon I have wondered who the Duke of Saldanha was, who has a section of Lisbon and a large square named after him. I discover from a little book that he organised a *coup d'état* in 1851 after a decade of coups and revolts. This is the way tourists grasp at unfamiliar history. The maps of most cities are abbreviated history textbooks. The street signs for the Rua Serpa Pinto are my first introduction to this famous explorer of Africa who crossed the continent from coast to coast in the 1870s. Chiado and Eça de Queiroz are new names to me, although they must be familiar to every educated Portuguese citizen.

Lisbon is an accumulation of centuries. The Luso-Roman cemetery and the Praça de Figueira built on top of it, the Castle with all its serial owners, the St Vincent da Fora Church on the site of a Crusaders' cemetery which was on the site of a monument to Vespasian – it is all modern Lisbon. Next week I am going to say good-bye to a friend with depths and complexities that I have barely begun to understand.

XIII

The Alfama, named by the Moors for some warm springs, is a delightful place. Strolling here is like exploring some eccentric old house with unexpected nooks and crannies. It is a neighbourhood of laundresses who hang their washing between the houses. Sometimes the passers-by are protected by a sheet of plastic under the washing, and sometimes not. A long flight of steps beside an ancient Visigothic wall ends in a narrow archway; around the corner you may find a fruit stall, a boy cleaning his motorbike or a dog sprawled in the sun. Women stand talking in dark doorways and children play tag through the maze of streets. Coming out into a *largo* is like finding a clearing in a forest. You can see a bigger patch of blue sky than the irregular ribbons of it that roof over the streets and the drying laundry. I am slightly disappointed if I loop back into a street or *largo* where I have been before; I want to wander through one new street after another. On a few of the larger streets there is even some motor traffic, including a tram route and two buses. A delivery truck is inching its way around a sharp corner on a hill. It would be easier to take out all the cans or apples and roll them down to the shop at the bottom of the street.

I come to the Miradouro de Santa Luzia, the patio where I came on the afternoon of the cremation. On a raised terrace above this patio is a little restaurant and café. Several people are sitting at outdoor tables enjoying the warm February sunshine. The checked tablecloths seem to pick up the pattern of the tessellated paving underfoot. Off to the south and west of this belvedere is the Tagus, bulging out into the broad Sea of Straw. Although the pergola is bare, I see the vines that have been cut back and will presumably cover it later in the season. On a day like this, filled with novelties and new sights, I think of Camus' character who says that there is so much to observe in one day of life that you could spend a hundred years in prison recalling your memories of it.

Finally I come down out of the Alfama on the river side onto the Cais de Santarem. It is a busy street with rattletrap trams racketing past, and its narrow sidewalks are crowded. I have not gone very far when I notice two men looking at me oddly and saying something to each other. They are talking about me, and I am immediately on my guard. They seem too well dressed and respectable to be bag-snatchers, and anyway, it is broad daylight on a busy street. No one has yet followed me or made romantic overtures, as happens several times a day to any woman tourist in Italy, so I suppose that sort of thing is not on their minds either, but what is?

They approach me and say something I can't catch. One of them actually reaches out and touches the strap of my shoulder bag! Can he be a bag-snatcher after all? This sedate-looking man in a business suit? Is this what all the warnings were about? Now, after years in London, the theft four years ago in Madrid, and all the warnings here, the most sensitive nerves I have are in my shoulder bag. I grip it tighter and demand testily, 'What do you want?'

'Ah, English,' he says. He motions to the other one, a fair-haired, well-built man, who is the English spokesman. I hope there is a good explanation for this.

'Your bag,' he says. 'Not safe here to carry the bag so. You should …' He runs out of words and mimes putting the bag strap over his head and wearing it across his chest. 'There are many unemployed here, and some, they … they …'

'Steal?' I suggest.

'Steal! Yes, they steal. So is not safe. You should carry it so,' and again he mimes putting the strap over his head.

‘Thank you,’ I say, and do as he suggests. So that was all they were talking about! They are pleasant and courteous men, and they only wanted to protect my passport and escudos, which are anyway in a purse on my belt. One is a lawyer and the other works for Portuguese customs. As we walk along on the crowded sidewalk, now three abreast, now single file, they impress upon me the danger of having one’s bag stolen by unemployed men loitering on the street.

‘The Alfama,’ the lawyer says, ‘the little streets,’ he gestures toward the way I have come. ‘They can steal,’ he says, miming a quick grab, ‘and go to those streets and you don’t see him again.’

‘Yes,’ says the customs inspector, ‘a foreign woman must be careful with the *bolsa.* You are English?’

‘American,’ I say.

‘I know someone at the American Embassy!’ he exclaims. ‘He is a friend of mine. Randolph Watson. We are …’ he looks mystified. He wants to say something he has thought of in his own language and he has discovered at the last moment that he doesn’t have the right word in English. He says something I don’t understand, including something about whistling. They whistle together? He takes out his wallet and removes a card from it. What the Portuguese customs officer and Watson at the embassy have in common is that they are both rugby referees. He shows me the card entitling him to referee matches in certain Portuguese rugby leagues.

‘Ah, rugby!’ I say, but as I know practically nothing about rugby, it’s my turn to be tongue-tied.

We walk on together until we come to a government building, where my two escorts stop. I shake hands with them both and thank them for their concern.

Not all of the people I invited can come for lunch, but John, Jaime and Mary Ann arrive at my hotel in a large Embassy limousine with smoked windows. We walk up to the Cervejaria da Trindade and are shown to our table in a smaller side gallery to the main cavern of the restaurant. This idea of taking them to lunch is exactly what would have occurred to Fern. That is not the reason I chose to do it myself, but I recognise a reflection of her approach in my own. It amuses me to think that I am doing what she would have done. It adds a little ironic cast to the proceedings.

From the start the luncheon is a very merry occasion. They all have a lively sense of humour and we four, all roughly the same age, seem to fall into a certain pattern of personalities as though we have been meeting for lunch every week for years. John, who is originally from Kansas, lived in Brazil for many years and is famous in the office for having seafood every day for lunch. True to form, he orders octopus today. Since I last saw John and Mary Ann and Jaime, I have thought of several questions I want to ask them. For one thing, what is the explanation for this custom of throwing eggs at strangers? They all look blank, even Jaime, who I was hoping could shed some light on this curious practice. It seems that not everything that happens in a foreign country is a foreign custom.

Another thing I keep noticing is people walking on crutches. I have imagined they were football injuries, but they can't all be. 'At first I thought it was because I was walking past a hospital, but then I saw them everywhere. They're both men and women, and all ages. One day I counted at least 20 people on crutches.'

'I am afraid,' says Jaime gravely, 'that my countrymen are not very careful. They take chances. They do things before they think about them.'

'In the car on the way here!' Mary Ann exclaims. 'A man with his leg in a cast was running through the traffic! He was on crutches with his leg sticking out in front. Four or five lanes of traffic and he was jaywalking straight through it! I couldn't believe it!'

Jaime nods in recognition. Yes, that's what he meant; that's what they do. 'We Portuguese,' says Jaime, 'trust God to protect us.'

'Yes,' retorts Mary Ann, 'and just look what a mess the rest of the world is in! It's because God is so busy with the Portuguese!'

Jaime begins to tell a story about some firemen who came to his apartment with a little folding ladder to use in getting into the apartment below his, but before he can go on the other two explain that the Portuguese fire departments all have a unit whose sole function is to help people get back into their apartments when they have locked themselves out. It was this unit that arrived at Jaime's door because the woman in the apartment below had locked herself out.

'They had a little ladder,' Jaime says.

'The ladder is *this* wide,' says Mary Ann, measuring six or eight inches with her hands.

'They told me they wanted to attach their ladder to my balcony,' says Jaime. 'They wanted to hook it over a flimsy little aluminum bar that would obviously have given way with the least pressure on the ladder. I said, "Oh no you're not!" and they said, "Oh yes we are!" My apartment is four storeys up! I wasn't going to have dead firemen on the sidewalk below! Not falling off *my* balcony!'

Jaime finally prevailed on the firemen to see reason, thereby saving their lives and amusing us hugely, and then John is reminded of a funny story about someone being careless on a balcony. When they first came to Lisbon they stayed somewhere temporarily before they found a permanent place to live. The landlady was about 90 and the 'girl' who acted as maid was not much younger.

'She knocked at the door,' says John, 'and said she had been sent to water the flowers. We said, "Yes, of course, come in." Then later we found her balancing on the railing of the balcony, watering all the hanging plants! She had taken her shoes off and climbed up on the railing, as she had no doubt been doing for the last 60 years! It worked on our nerves. We really couldn't let her do it again. So we told the landlady that *we* would look after the plants!'

It is light, amusing table conversation; it is a ballgame with no score, played for the love of handling the ball. We have serious comments, hilarious anecdotes, and casual observations. We have enquiries, surmises, and reminiscences. These three people all work in the same place, but for a couple of hours they include me in their jokes and gossip. I for my part ask them probing questions which prompt illuminating remarks and stories. I am the unknown quantity, known until now only as a persistent letter writer, a client with a grievance. They inhabit a world where travel is by limousine with smoked windows, and I intersect them for the moment with my own world of the inquisitive tourist.

We talk about the architecture in Brasilia, where John was last posted. Mary Ann's first posting was in Paris, an enormous embassy with several diplomats of ambassadorial rank. Later she went to Barranquilla, where she learned to fire a machine gun. 'It was the centre of the illegal drug business,' she remarks by way of explanation. Then she tells an amusing story about how, quite unexpectedly, her knowledge of Greek, left over from the Athens posting, came in handy when she was sent to Brazil.

I ask how often they have to go back to the United States. There are rather complicated rules. They are allowed annual leave, which may be spent anywhere, and home leave, which must be spent in the United States. They are sent home every two or three years.

'Do you have culture shock when you go back?' I ask.

'Yes!' says Mary Ann. 'The last time I went back I heard a talking cash register! The voice called out the price and I looked all around …'

This is the first I've ever heard of talking cash registers, but then nobody sends me on home leave to keep up with these things. 'Talking cash registers?' I say.

'You feel so stupid,' says Mary Ann.

'Don't you have them in England?' John asks. I have to

admit that we don't, even at the big modern supermarket near where I live. This is an experience I have to look forward to.

We talk about learning foreign languages. Jaime is sure that certain people are incapable of learning foreign languages. The British and American people who have retired to Portugal never learn a word of Portuguese. I point out that there are so many of them that they can talk to each other for a long time before they need to learn Portuguese to talk to anybody else.

'You, for instance,' Jaime says to Mary Ann, 'you look like such a typical American, and yet you speak Portuguese. I was surprised the first time I heard you speaking Portuguese.'

It is hard to explain to Europeans, crowded together on their peninsula, that until fairly recently most Americans hardly needed to learn foreign languages with a view to speaking them with foreigners. When and where were they likely to meet foreigners? 'Anyone who got as far as Kansas,' I say, turning to John, 'would already speak English.' Jaime laughs, and I go on to tell him that until recently – 'recently' being my own school days in the 50s and 60s – Latin was the most widely taught foreign langauge in American schools. I tell him this because I know he will be surprised. Jaime is gratifyingly amazed that a country which doesn't speak a Romance language should study Latin at all.

I tell them that I have seen a truck unloading dried codfish at a restaurant and – this is my punchline – the fish were from Norway! Mary Ann and John laugh, but Jaime is not surprised. Of course they are imported. 'After '74,' he says, 'our balance of payments situation was so bad that we couldn't afford to import *bacalhau* any more.' He shudders slightly at the memory. 'It was a terrible time for us.' Jaime is eating *bacalhau* now, I'm glad to see.

Our table is as animated and merry as any of the tables in the evening, when groups of people meet in the Cervejaria da Trindade for food and conversation. We are not raucous, so as to cause everyone to turn around to see who is making all the noise, but there must be an atmosphere of merriment for several yards around our table here in this side gallery by the big windows. Fern would have enjoyed this. It's a great pity that Jaime, John and Mary Ann never met Fern. It's almost as though they did know her, though, because they are as kind and obliging as they would have been if they had known her personally. They would have liked her, certainly, and she would have been interested in their experiences and amused by their stories.

Mary Ann says that in the State Department in Washington they say that you can always tell a woman who works in the Foreign Service: she is wearing loads of gold jewelry and a Sears Roebuck dress! I picture this anonymous woman in her mail-order dress and her chunky 18-carat rings and necklaces arriving at the State Department from some dangerous and primitive place. We all laugh uproariously, even though the others must have heard it before. What camaraderie they all seem to have! How kind of them to share it briefly with me. Why didn't I think of joining the Foreign Service? Now I might know Greek and possess lots of gold jewelry. But I remember the machine-gun drill in Colombia, and my imaginary career is nipped in the bud.

It is extraordinary that I am sitting here with these three people, drinking coffee after a good lunch in this restaurant in Lisbon, just because my mother died here seven years ago. It is a ridiculous turn of events. That's the only word for it: 'ridiculous'. Suppose we had gone to Greece instead? Suppose she had died a week earlier when we were in Granada? Sometimes I think she would have found the situation comical, except for the parts of it that have been painful for me. She would regard the whole idiotic business as 'an interesting experience'. Death itself didn't seem to frighten her at all. 'Oh, is this it?' she seemed to say. 'Well then, this is it.' It was part of her invincible dignity. She went 'gentle into that good night', because it would have been out of character to rage against it.

'Heigh-ho!' she used to say, and it had a remarkable range of meanings. It meant 'What an ironic/ludicrous/unexpected situation with what absurd/unpleasant/unforeseen implications.' It meant 'Here we go again' and 'Nothing ventured, nothing gained' and 'Oh dear, how is this going to turn out?' 'Heigh-ho!' would have been the response when, at different times in her life, unexpected things of varying seriousness happened. It was 'Heigh-ho!' when her children at New Winchester left a dead mouse in her desk one April Fool's Day or when the pilot light of the furnace at the Old Brick House went out on Christmas Eve. The choir director has the 'flu? North opens the bidding in no trump? Ayres doesn't have the beige voile dress in her size? Heigh-ho. Or it's already August and she still hasn't found a teaching job? Heigh-ho. And heigh-ho, a divorce looks inevitable.

Lying on that bed in the Hotel Valverde, she might easily have thought 'Heigh-ho' as she lost consciousness, it seems to me. Is this trivialising her or death? Possibly, but the point is that it was not frightening, even though she had other plans which did not include it. 'If this is a heart attack, that's all right,' is what she actually said, and that's not so far removed from 'Heigh-ho'. So, Death, where is thy sting? It's the survivors who get stung, not the people like Fern who calmly look Death in the eye and stare it down.

Finally the Embassy people begin to look at their watches. They have to get back to work out at Sete Rios. I pay the bill and we go out onto the street to look for the car and driver. We chat for a moment in the Largo da Trindade before the car appears. I'm really sorry to see them go. I've enjoyed this leisurely Continental lunch with them more than I can say. They all get into the big Chevrolet with darkened windows and disappear even before the car drives off.

I have now finished all possible business in Lisbon. I have a sensation of things being complete. I have substantially finished what I came to do, which was to have the cremation, thank the people who have helped me, and see as much as possible of the city. I came here to explore Lisbon and explore myself. I came to think about my mother and her death, here where I saw her last.

XIV

I filled the notebook I brought with me and had to buy another. Now I'm jotting things in it at night or when I stop for a meal or coffee. I am already looking forward to coming back to Lisbon the next time. I have still not been to the Madre de Deus church or the Naval Museum. After I bought a ticket for the revue at the Laura Alves Theatre, the performance was cancelled. Not everything worked out according to plan. There were train strikes, or I might have gone farther afield from Lisbon. As it was, I went to Sintra one day and back in the evening past the floodlit Aguas Livres aqueduct across the Alcântara Valley. I have walked startling distances through the city. Later, plotting them on the map using the position of the hotel and the Metro lines as a guide, I am struck both by how far I've walked and by how much more there is to explore.

Last night on my way down to the hotel bar for a bottle of cold mineral water, I passed the door of the television lounge. A comedy sketch was on: a courtroom scene with a comical defendant in drag and a hectoring judge who seemed to be losing a battle of wits with the defendant. It was a familiar kind of skit, even though I couldn't understand the words. One of the hotel maids was standing in the doorway laughing at it, going into fresh giggles with each wisecrack from the posturing defendant. She was enjoying it so much that I knew it must be funny. But I found her more interesting to watch than the comedy sketch. I knew she had spent a hard day making beds and cleaning bathtubs, and it was nice to watch her enjoying herself. Once or twice something was so funny that she clapped her hands in delight. I couldn't help wondering if anyone had ever died in *her* hotel. Had *she* ever knocked on a door to express her condolences?

As I get older my mother gets younger. I am now about the age she was when I was a toddler. When I look back on her life at that time with my perspective on my own life, I can guess at her problems and difficulties. There were financial anxieties and the recent divorce; there were efforts to find a job, raise two children and look after a house full of lodgers. She had invaluable help and support from her family, but it can't have been easy. I have none of these problems, and I wonder whether I could cope with them all at once. I'm inclined to think not.

As a toddler, what did I notice? Not much. I hadn't seen much of my father during the marriage, and now that he was officially absent there wasn't much difference. Adults were mysterious beings in any case, who conducted their conversations in the watches of the night when children were asleep in their high-sided cribs. I slept to a background hum of lowered voices in distant rooms where lights still burned; from nearer rooms the light cast a slant yellow door shape on the floor.

Now that I am the age she was then, I see her as something like a contemporary. I might be one of her woman friends to whom she confided on the telephone at the desk in the stairwell. I might hear of the necessity for the divorce; of the job interview where she had been told she was too old (she with a little girl of four!); of the dangerous Lombardy poplar that was going to have to be cut down.

As I grow older and my mother keeps pace, our lives will form fleeting parallels. When I am 50 or 55 or 60, I will have a whole set of new insights into her life at those ages. I didn't have this feeling very strongly until after she died. At her death, her life became a whole with a clear beginning and end. It took on a special shape that it hadn't had while she was still living it. It was now possible to say exactly what the mid-point was. After she died it occurred to me that people who knew her only later in life were missing out on important elements of the story. It is ironic that I should feel this way, who knew her only in the second half of her life. I at least had old pictures, family stories, and her diaries to guide me. Some people still living had known her in a way I never could – as a young woman, her hair still brown, her stride strong and tireless. They may recall her driving an old Marmon, the side curtains flapping in the wind of 40 miles an hour. She was sporty, carrying her wooden tennis racket with the elongated 1920s shape. She sat at the upright piano in a smart dress and amber beads, so that people would remember the effect she made and tell me about it 30 and 40 years later.

It is again a pleasure to think about her and her life. After she died it was painful, but then during the following year the grief slowly wore off. Now, after the acute attack of grief at the cremation, I am again able to think of her without pain. It is very strange how this works. It seems to depend entirely on time – the stuff you can measure but not define – which does not heal all wounds, as the saying has it, but is only a bandage that can slip. The scar tissue is a provisional patch with a way of dissolving and spilling out the blood again.

I am out by the big, red, Moorish-looking bullring at Campo Pequeno. I have just crossed a busy street and see a blind man tapping toward me with his white cane. When I have seen blind people on street corners before in Lisbon, someone has always appeared in a moment to help them cross. There is no one else anywhere near, except the group of people waiting for a bus behind me on the other side of the street. I realise with a mixture of anticipation and dread that *I* am the member of the public fated to help this blind man. He is elderly and stooped and stands tapping his cane on the kerbstone, waiting for me. The road is clear, so I take his elbow and say, '*Agora, senhor.*' Now. We reach the island in the middle of the street, and some cars are coming on that side. Suddenly I realise that

I have made a terrible mistake in offering to be a Good Samaritan: I don't know how to say 'Stop'! I don't know the word for 'wait'!

I pull at his sleeve as the cars approach. 'Stop,' I finally say, conscious that I am botching my attempt at helpfulness. He calls out to the air in general, asking if this is where the bus goes. The bus queue now come to his rescue and mine and call to him that yes, this is the place; yes, this is where the bus stops; yes, it is safe to come toward them now. I am relieved to let go of the blind man's sleeve – relieved that the bus queue has now taken over the responsibility that I had tried to assume. Now, crossing the street for the third time, I escape in the opposite direction and leave the bus queue and its new member behind me. I would have done him a favour by not trying to do him a favour. It is as though the Good Samaritan had put the injured man on his donkey and then let him fall off. Perhaps the priest and the Levite knew what they were doing when they passed by on the other side.

The Rua Augusta is closed to traffic nowadays, and this sidewalk café has extended itself out into the street, where my table is sitting on a disused and rather silted-up tram track. Down to the left at the end of the Rua Augusta is the huge triumphal arch that gives onto Black Horse Square, also called the Praça do Comércio, also called Terreira do Paço, where the first equestrian statue in Portugal still stands. I'm having a cold drink; it's hot in the direct sunlight. A child of about four comes up to me with a fistful of Band-Aids to sell. '*Obrigada, não*,' I say, hoping to be civil but not encouraging.

This whole street, as I sit here near the top and looking down the length of it, is actually flat. Lisboans must come here for the novelty of walking up and down on a level surface. Certainly there are a lot of shoppers and strollers out on this Saturday afternoon. I have just made up my mind to go and get a little book in Portuguese about the history of the

Discoveries. I shall get it at the Ferin bookshop on the Rua Nova do Almada. I've passed the shop several times and seen the book in the window. The first time I saw the name of the shop from a distance, I thought for a moment it said 'Fern'.

For the moment it is pleasant to sit here watching the people walk past. I shall miss all this. I wonder if this is what very old people feel about dying. I want to write about it. I want to describe this flat street with the dusty tram track down the middle and the imposing monument at the end. I want to describe Lisbon: the way the light falls through the palm trees and the bare plane trees with their paint-by-numbers bark on the Avenida da Liberdade; the look of the arches of the ruined Carmo church high above the city and the black and white arabesques underfoot; the feel of the warm sun on my back at a sidewalk café table and the sound of the language in the streets.

I ask the waiter for a cup of espresso coffee, and I eat a tangerine with it. The sun is moving around behind the buildings on the other side of this narrow street, and as a result the shadow has moved onto the chair opposite me, like a guest at my table. As I enumerate the pleasures of being in Lisbon I see that writing about them, that is, the act of recalling them and describing them on paper, will be a pleasure in itself. Now that it is a pleasure to think of Fern again, I want to describe her, too. I want to describe Fern to people who never knew her so that they will have an idea of her life and her character. Is it possible nowadays to present one's mother as an admirable person without sounding mawkish? And who am I to try it? After all, I am sprung from a family that collects significant tree bark.

Perhaps it may help people through their own rough patches when the grief seems interminable. Like a fado, the whole story may be melancholy in parts, but not altogether depressing. *Grave, ma non troppo*. Like a fado, it will celebrate Lisbon.

Now the sun is beginning to throw a grey cloth over my

little table. February himself, the old masher, puts a frosty hand on my knee. This café has the lease of the sun for the morning only. I pay for my drinks and walk on, up some narrow streets, back down other narrow streets, through little *largos* and big squares. I buy the little book about the Portuguese Discoveries and carry it with me in a plastic bag advertising the Ferin Bookshop, founded in 1840. I buy a twist of roasted chestnuts in a cone of the *Yellow Pages*. The salty charcoal chestnut taste has lost its London associations and is now pure Lisbon.

Later, on the Avenida da Liberdade, I am at the charming café where three long rows of glass-topped, white wrought-iron tables extend down the esplanade, each with four white wrought-iron chairs. I take out my notebook and lay it on the glass-topped table. There are patterns in the story that I didn't invent. They are just there, like the black arabesques on the off-white sidewalk.

It's taking shape as I sit here at the wrought-iron table under the palm trees. It will be a record of things that really happened. There will have to be a section about Mother, but where shall I start? Some people will find a small-town music teacher inherently uninteresting. The idea of Christian commitment may seem merely dull to some. Who will take my word for it that she was neither uninteresting nor dull?

I once showed a sample of Fern's handwriting, anonymously, to a friend who is a graphologist. The graphologist had not been very interested in the two or three samples of other people's writing I had just shown her. ('Typical neurotic handwriting,' she had said, glancing at them and handing them back.) But she looked carefully at Fern's. I have said it was distinctive. It was not a scribble but not straight from the copybook, either. The letters were clear and well formed, with firm strokes. 'This is very interesting,' the graphologist said slowly. 'This person has a really strong centre – something that gives her strength. It could be religion, but it doesn't have to be. This is *very* interesting handwriting. May I keep it for my collection?' When I assented she tucked the page of writing carefully into her bag.

I don't know quite what this strong centre might have been, besides religion. The perseverance of the Chambers and the stoical calm of the Reeds, perhaps. (One of her father's pioneer ancestors, treed by wolves, had tied himself to some branches and settled down for the night. What did *his* handwriting look like?) The strength she acquired from meeting challenges. Whatever it was, she must have had it at a fairly early age, because her handwriting hardly changed for 50 years. It got more regular and compact, but the letter forms were there in her 1924 diary. She must remain partly a mystery to me, although we often had an intuitive understanding of each other.

I shall offset all this solemn stuff with descriptions of her funny side. It will be hard to get it all in, and in the right balance. Her sense of enjoyment. How she loved a good blizzard any time, but especially on her birthday! She really didn't mind being snowbound, as long as the ice didn't break the electricity lines – even then I think she still enjoyed it. She always liked candlelight, whether we were snowbound or not. I must try to give an accurate impression of her life before I was born; I must get all those schools where she taught in the right order. When did she teach in Stockton, Illinois? ('The year I was out in Stockton …' she would say, but what year was that?) Other bits of the story will have to be told partly from a child's point of view, because that is what I remember.

I look up into the trees around the café and flex my writing hand. She is with me in all sorts of subtle ways. Sometimes I catch myself cocking my head to one side the way she used to at the movies. Is it in the genes or what?

The waiter has come and gone with glasses and cups. It will be time to leave before long. I just have a couple more ideas to jot down in my notebook. I will begin the story as I arrive in Lisbon. I might as well begin with the plane coming down at the Lisbon airport. Then I will get myself to the hotel in the Rua Garrett with the taxi driver who asked if I had come to see the shrine at Fátima. In the beginning it will not be clear why I have come to this place. Then later I will describe the events at the Hotel … I must think of some other name for that hotel. And a different name for the anatomy teacher at the medical school. Maybe he had some reason for not writing. Maybe what he knew was too complicated to try to express in English.

Fern would say, 'Good night! If I'd known you'd be put to all this trouble I would have made some other arrangements. Still, I expect in some ways it's been an interesting experience.'

Works Consulted or Cited

Andersen, Hans Christian, *A Visit to Portugal 1866* (trans. Grace Thornton), London, 1972

Atkinson, William C., *A History of Spain and Portugal*, Harmondsworth, 1960

Bradford, Sarah, *Portugal*, London, 1973

Bridge, Ann and Susan Lowndes, *The Selective Traveller in Portugal*, London, 1949

Brophy, Brigid, 'Lisbon: City As Art' in *Reads*, London, 1989

Calderon Dinis, Alberto Maria, *História de Lisboa*, Lisboa, [1947]

Cameron, Ian, *Magellan and the First Circumnavigation of the World*, London, 1974

Camoens, Luis Vaz de, *The Lusiads* (trans. William C. Atkinson), Harmondsworth, 1952

Cheke, Marcus, *Dictator of Portugal: A Life of the Marquis of Pombal 1699-1782*, London, 1938

Cheke, Marcus, 'The Portuguese Character' in *Portugal and Brazil* (ed. H.V. Livermore), Oxford, 1953

Clavell, Xavier Costa, *All Lisbon and its Surroundings*, 8th ed., Barcelona, 1986

Clyne, Douglas, *Your Guide to Portugal*, London, 1965

Crofton, Ian, *Concise Dictionary of Music*, London, 1986

Entwhistle, William J., 'The Portuguese and Brazilian Language' in *Portugal and Brazil* (ed. H.V. Livermore), Oxford, 1953

Evans, David J.J., *Portugal*, London, 1990

Fodor's Lisbon Guide 1985, New York, 1985
Freitas da Costa, Eduardo, *Efemérides de história de Portugal.*, 2nd ed., Lisboa, 1950
Gaziel, *Portugal lejano*, Barcelona, 1964
Green, J.C.R., *Fernando Pessoa: The Genesis of the Heteronyms*, Portree, 1982
Inchbold, A.C., *Lisbon and Cintra*, London, 1907
Leão, F. da Cunha, *O enigma Português*, Lisboa, 1973
Leça, Armando, *Da Música Portuguêsa*, Lisboa, 1922
Livermore, H.V., *A History of Portugal*, Cambridge, 1947
Livermore, H.V. (ed.), *Portugal and Brazil*, Oxford, 1953
Livermore, H.V., *Portugal, a Short History*, Edinburgh, 1973
Macaulay, Rose, *They Went to Portugal,* Harmondsworth, 1986 (1st ed. 1946)
Marden, Philip S., *A Wayfarer in Portugal*, London, 1927
Myhill, Henry, *Portugal*, London, 1972
Oliveira, Luna de, *Timor na história de Portugal* (3 vols.), Lisboa, 1949
Pessoa, Fernando, *Selected Poems* (trans. Jonathan Griffin), 2nd ed., Harmondsworth, 1982
Pimentel, Alberto, *A triste canção do sul*, Lisboa, 1904
Prestage, Edgar, *The Portuguese Pioneers*, London, 1933
Prestage, Edgar, 'Vasco da Gama' in *The Dublin Review*, April 1926
Ribeiro, Orlando, *A Formação de Portugal*, Lisboa, 1987
Ricklefs, M.C., *A History of Modern Indonesia*, London, 1981
Rio, João do, *Fados e canções do Portugal*, Rio de Janeiro [1909]
Sadie, Stanley (ed.), *The New Grove Dictionary of Music and Musicians*, London, 1980
Wohl, Helmut and Alice Wohl, *Portugal,* London, 1983

The quotation on p.117 is from 'Chicago' by Carl Sandburg in Carl Sandburg, *Complete Poems* (New York, 1950). The quotation on p.105 is a modernised version of one stanza of the medieval lyric 'Timor mortis conturbat me' ('The fear of death distresses me'). It appears in various collections, but the one I have used is Robert D. Stevick (ed.), *One Hundred Middle English Lyrics* (Indianapolis and New York, 1964).